BEYOND CELL MEMORY

BEYOND CELL MEMORY

Messages from Creator on Origin, Purpose and Use of
DNA and Cell Memory

GRACE J. SCOTT

iUniverse, Inc.
Bloomington

BEYOND CELL MEMORY
MESSAGES FROM CREATOR ON ORIGIN, PURPOSE AND USE OF DNA AND CELL MEMORY

The views expressed in this work are solely those of the author and do not necessarily reflect the views of the publisher, and the publisher hereby disclaims any responsibility for them.

iUniverse books may be ordered through booksellers or by contacting:

iUniverse
1663 Liberty Drive
Bloomington, IN 47403
www.iuniverse.com
1-800-Authors (1-800-288-4677)

Because of the dynamic nature of the Internet, any web addresses or links contained in this book may have changed since publication and may no longer be valid.

Any people depicted in stock imagery provided by Thinkstock are models, and such images are being used for illustrative purposes only.
Certain stock imagery © Thinkstock.

ISBN: 978-1-4620-3714-8 (sc)
ISBN: 978-1-4620-3713-1(hc)
ISBN: 978-1-4620-3712-4 (ebk)

Library of Congress Control Number: 2011911885

Printed in the United States of America

iUniverse rev. date: 08/11/2011

Contents

To all members of my family and extended family, in the present and in the Beyond, who have encouraged and supported my endeavors

Acknowledgments

I feel deeply honored and humbled to have received this highly spiritual information. I thank our Creator for sending the information. Also, I thank Him for the elevated souls He selected for messengers. Their loyalty and dedication to Creator enabled them to complete the mission of channeling material to help souls on Earth. I am thankful for my friend and reflexologist, the gifted Naomi, who channeled the information. In concert with these efforts, I have recorded and typed the words given and clarified anything that was not clear, which was my assignment. This mission ends with the completion of this third book.

Who is Naomi? Naomi is a gifted reflexologist. She has gifts of prophecy, channeling, healing, and dream interpretation. She said that at a young age, she told her parents to leave the house it was going to burn. The parents removed the children from the house and the house did indeed burn. By training, Naomi is a certified Reflexologist and gets paid for that work, not the channeling.

Because of her gift, she is the human channel through which souls from the Other Side or dimensions speak. They all speak by thought. Many souls don't know English so they use a machine that converts their thoughts to English. The accuracy rate of the material received is eighty-six percent, according to those that channel. Usually if errors or questions occur, someone channels to correct the problem. Only the Creator is perfect is stated often.

Naomi does not know when or if any soul will appear to channel. She can't access anyone on demand. When channeling does occur, she does not recall what she channeled. Every three months she schedules a Gathering, which is an open session for a group of people. During the Gathering, several people usually channel to the group and to individuals.

Those who attend usually leave a donation. Naomi is a generous soul. Often, she treats people and refuses payment.

People have asked how I managed to write these books. First, the channeled material came through Naomi. When the channeling started in 2002, I knew how to type. I knew how to write term papers and procedure manuals. I did not know how to use a computer or how to begin writing a book. Eventually, my husband taught me to use his computer and then bought one for me. He deserves a lot of credit for his time and patience as I worked on this project. Also, he deserves credit for hours spent on maintenance of computers and supplies. His intelligence, occasional proofreading and suggestions were most helpful. He was completely supportive of this long project.

My daughter, a professional writer, was a big help with the first book, even though she lives far from me. When I presented her with hundreds of typed pages and asked her opinion, her first thought had to be, "Bonfire." But, being a kind soul, she outlined what I needed to do with the pile of typed pages to get a manuscript. A few thousand hours later and more revisions, she received my manuscript and designed a book format. Using the Select package information provided by iUniverse, the publisher, I stumbled my way through the publishing process.

My son provided confirmation of personality and character traits of those he had known that crossed over on 9/11/2001. Also, he encouraged the continued recording and publishing of the channeled information. He recognized it as something important that I must do.

My daughter recommended the publisher iUniverse. She had read one of their books and liked the quality of the work. For my first book I chose their Select package, for the second book I chose Bookstore Premier Pro and for the third book I chose Online Premier Pro. I have learned a great deal by following the their material published online and through talking with staff. Writing a book, even when the most of the material is channeled, is a very tedious, time consuming project. It can be frustrating. It is also an expensive undertaking.

A few times, I had concerns about what was channeled on a subject. Having been told in channeling that all such books come from the Other Side, I read what famous authors had to say on the subject in question. This helped me accept what was said and proceed onward.

For the third book, I found support by reviewing books I'd read years before by Sylvia Browne, Edgar Cayce, Deepak Chopra and many others. While finishing the cell memory book, I became stuck in the third part. For some reason, I thought of the books of Gary Zukav sitting on my shelves. I started to read them. I went to his website and heard him speak of letting the thoughts flow. At another point, the same thing happened and I was led to *The Divine Matrix* by Gregg Braden and later to *Same Soul, Many Bodies* by Dr. Brian L. Weiss.

Then through channeled material I was led to a person who referred me to books of Dr. William Frist, Michael Newton, Bruce Lipton, Brandon Bays and Scott Degenhardt. I bought them all. I started reading. I found that the channeled material I had received fit with some of the research these authors have done and, in some instances, fills the "gaps" of which some of them have spoken. I used endnotes to cite the quotes I used from some of the books. These books helped me return to that space inside where thoughts flow freely and I write. I do receive assistance from souls of the Other Side sometimes. They call it "knowledge infusion." I thank all of you for your hard work.

Most recently, I was amazed to receive clearly channeled thoughts myself. In a dream, a former boss clearly appeared, spoke, and gave me gold earrings. As I awoke and got out of bed, he continued to speak clearly by thought. I sat down and quietly wrote his words. Then I went to my appointment with Naomi. He met me there and said: This was a practice session. I wasn't finished speaking. He said that on the Other Side, he assists doctors working on cell memory research. He provides them with items they request for their work. Now, when others are busy, he will bring messages from the doctors to me for the book. The practice session was to see if I received accurately. I did.

We all have the capacity to receive if we are open and practice. I was astounded at the clarity of his message and the clarity of his personality.

The words chosen and the personality matched the man I had known in the eighties. Such communication by thought is what is supposed to happen to many people on Earth as the changes progress. Telepathic communication existed as the first communication among souls and Creator. We're encouraged to relearn and return to this process. Why? Power outages following disasters and cataclysmic events will disable our present systems of communication awhile.

Preface

Beyond Cell Memory is the culmination of three books of channeled material. The channeling began about six months after terrorists attacked the United States 9/11/2001 and has not ceased. That attack by those of evil intentions and evil energies opened the door of no return for accelerated Earth cleansing. The battles that have ensued are battles between good and evil. As stated from the outset, the battles will end by the hand of God, not man. Earth's geography and the people that survive will be forever changed by a major cataclysm. Survivors will number thousands, not millions.

In preparation for this cataclysm and events that follow, the most recent messages sent by Creator are to accurately inform all souls of their origin—how he made souls and why they have cell memory and DNA. The messages are given in simple language so that all may read and understand that every soul on Earth and every soul on other planetary systems were made by the same Creator and have DNA and cell memory from the Creator.

Why give this information now? Humans have been misinformed about their creation and all the planning that goes into how each soul arrives upon Earth. Correct information is very necessary because of cataclysmic Earth changes that are rapidly approaching. Many people will not survive the cataclysm, and they need to know what happens when they leave Earth and not have fear. This information is to help them understand what is happening and where they will be going. They need to understand how to clear traumatic cell memories before crossing. Hopefully, this will allow them to clear traumatic and negative cell memories before leaving Earth.

For those who remain through the cataclysm and assist others, the information is to help those who assist and those who survive. Both categories need to prepare and be aware of what to expect. Creator sends this information for individuals to read, digest and apply. For souls that remain in the physical body after the cataclysm, this information is to aid their physical survival, help them make decisions and help the soul clear traumatic cell memories. For example, some people may have traumatic cell memories from loss of limbs, cuts and bruises and loss of family.

The information also addresses some of the most controversial topics now battled on Earth: homosexuality, abortions, suicide, and organ transplants. DNA and cell memory also connect these issues in our daily life and back to how things were designed to work.

Also, for souls that have chosen to leave Earth, the topics covered are how a soul's chart is developed—including its points of entry and exit of Earth. We have five chosen exit points that we may opt to take. This information is to help individual souls cleanse cell memory while on this side and grow spiritually in the process. Doing this also shortens the cell memory cleansing process when the soul leaves the body and arrives in the cleansing chambers on the Other Side. There, the life just lived is reviewed and the soul feels whatever it caused others to feel. This may be a long and painful process, depending upon the life one lived.

Creator chose highly elevated souls to deliver his messages. These souls and their areas include the following: Jamiah, humble and loyal servant to Creator and God of Earth; Oshinbah, Ambassador who oversees the universes and planetary systems; Elijah, Assistant to Oshinbah, and former marine/police sergeant who gave it all on 9/11/2001; Edgar Cayce, formerly known on Earth as the Sleeping Prophet; and Celonious—Head of a council that oversees charts planned by souls who request a life on Earth. These are the primary speakers with channeled material from Creator. Athena, my spirit guide for this lifetime, deserves special recognition for her incredible efforts, loyalty, and dedication.

The messages were channeled through the gifted Naomi, a reflexologist. Naomi says that she was born with the gifts of prophecy, dream interpretation and healing. I, the author, digitally recorded the messages spoken through Naomi. I then typed, assembled, proofread and published the material as requested. I have tried to keep the material received intact. This is not my field of expertise.

Information in this book is divided into parts:

Part I: Origin, Purpose and Use of DNA and Cell Memory

Messengers carefully selected by Creator deliver His messages on the origin, function and use of DNA and cell memory. Creator sent Jamiah, Oshinbah, Celonious and Edgar Cayce to deliver these messages. The messages were delivered in simple words from Creator.

Part II: DNA and Cell Memory Connections

In this section, Edgar Cayce speaks about visions and dreams. Sir Isaac Newton reveals that DNA and cell memory are connected to all universes and planetary systems.

Dr. Sigmund Freud speaks about dream work and cell memory. Cell memories may present as emotional garbage or manifest as a physical problem or disease. To heal the physical, these must be recognized and cleared in the soul. For examples of such clearing, Sigmund Freud gave this author dreams over several months. He then interpreted the dreams by speaking through the gifted Naomi, a reflexologist. This was done to clear "my emotional garbage," which was necessary for me to do before writing this third book and before the earth cleansing takes place.

And in subsequent chapters, Carl Jung speaks about homosexuality, and Jamiah and Edgar Cayce speak about abortions and suicide. One chapter is devoted to organ transplant cases in which cell memories of the donor manifest in the recipient. Cell memory is the thread that connects all of these topics. Cell memory exists on Earth and all planetary systems.

Part III: Using Cell Memory to Heal

An overview contains *new information* about the energy of Creator and His/Her creations. Initially, Jamiah and Makala appeared to bring the new information. Jamiah is masculine energy; his counterpart is Makala, a feminine energy. After years of working with this channeled material, I finally asked this question: Why does Jamiah sometimes say that he reports to Creator and at other times, he says he reports to God? The answer was quite complex. With Jamiah's consent, Makala responded.

The Creator made the universes, galaxies and planetary systems and all the planetary system inhabitants. He placed one God over each planetary system. There is one God over the planetary system that contains Earth, Jupiter, Mars and the other planets. Each of the other planetary systems also has a God in charge of that system. There are other energy densities that serve Creator and God. (We, on Earth, would call the densities a hierarchy of reporting, or an organizational structure.) Makala referred to the energies as densities.

The creation of the Mother God and Father God was so that each soul might experience all that is of a masculine nature and all that is of the feminine nature and grow spiritually. This ability to experience allows the soul to balance, and souls must be balanced to return to Creator. However, when the physical dies and the soul is free to return, most souls do not go back directly to Creator. Most go instead to the God over their own planet of origin and no further. A reason given for this is that most souls of Earth think that when we pray to God we are praying to the highest of high. Actually, Creator is the highest of high energy and He/She made everything else. Makala spent two sessions explaining the roles of energy densities.

Also found in this section are the methods given in channeling for clearing cell memory problems. These methods are hypnosis, meditation, and dream work. The soul contains all cell memories of all lives we have ever lived; this includes the present life. Some people have lived traumatic lives and stored the memories of these in the soul. It is possible to access these memories, identify the problem, let the problem go, and in doing this, heal the soul of the trauma. Some people are able to bring forth these memories in meditation and dreams. Very difficult cases may require a psychiatrist that practices regressive hypnosis.

The energy we work with is that of Creator. Whether we undergo hypnosis, do meditation or record dreams, we are working with the energy of the Creator and our own souls. In channeling, we've learned that we are all energy and for our protection, we need to surround ourselves with light regularly. Simple instruction for how to do this is given.

An important element in advancing our spiritual growth while here on Earth is our ability to clear negative and traumatic memories whether they are from this life or from prior lives. Many of these are the source of our mental and physical ailments. Clearing the negative cell memories through dreams, hypnosis and meditation often heals a person.

I hope you find this information helpful.

Introduction

Since February of 2002, I have been the recipient of material channeled through Naomi. The information is channeled thoughts by souls. Creator chose the messages to be published at this time. Also, Creator chose trusted, elevated souls to deliver the messages. Of the souls that channeled, some souls once lived in human bodies on Earth, for example Edgar Cayce and Elijah. Others, such as Jamiah, Oshinbah, and Celonious have never lived on Earth.

The primary purpose of the channeled material—at this time—is to help humans attain rapid spiritual growth and prepare for cataclysmic Earth changes, which are imminent. Since the events of 9/11/2001, information channeled through Naomi has produced three books to assist others through the difficult years that have occurred and those that are yet to come.

Following the 9/11/2001 attacks on New York and Washington, D.C., Al Qaeda leaders proudly proclaimed success in accomplishing their goal to kill as many Americans as possible. Most of the terrorists identified were of Arab origin and claimed to be of the Muslim religion. In their heinous acts, they killed members of various races, including their own, from around the world. Their evil acts opened the door of no return for the cleansing of the Earth.

Their evil is of the same nature as the first energy of evil that entered the Earth eons ago. It has grown over time through numerous evil leaders and other individuals and now, has almost overcome the good of Earth. This evil grew by souls misusing the free will the Creator gave them.

Earth is in the process of cleansing. This has been discussed at length in the previous two books. Around 2012 a major cataclysm is to occur.

Millions of humans have charted to leave Earth at this time. Survival will be of utmost interest to those who have charted to remain. It is hoped that the information will be accepted, absorbed, and applied to clearing traumatic cell memories. This clears the soul and aids healing of the physical human body. Also, clearing of cell memories while on Earth enables the soul to clear faster when it leaves Earth. Cleansing allows the soul to quickly go on to other assignments or reincarnate.

Part of the cleansing process that we are witnessing is the increase in number and severity of natural disasters. These will increase in severity as Earth prepares for the Great Lakes to empty into the Mississippi River and a massive tsunami wipes out New York City and most of the state. As has been given, most of the shorelines will be gone and in many areas have already changed from rising water levels. Follow and observe the paths of natural disasters. These are the paths given for the cataclysmic events. Now, this has been a peek at the background that led to the present book.

Beyond Cell Memory focuses on the origin, use and function of DNA and cell memory. The focus involves the emotional aspects of Earth as a planet and how emotions are connected to our spiritual growth, cell memory, and many health problems. Souls come here to experience and learn emotions. Love, compassion, empathy, and forgiveness are examples of positive emotions. Anger, fear, hate, are examples of negative emotions.

Earth is also known as the only planet with the soul living inside a living organism called human. Earth is also the current school of learning opportunities for all planetary systems. This is one reason it is overpopulated. Souls desire to come here for the access to rapid spiritual growth. Opportunities offered on Earth are not available on most other planets.

Certain criteria apply to material that is received by channeling. Information from the Other Side is given only as fast as the receiver is able to grasp, accept, and digest it. The receiver must understand and accept what is given because doubt stalls or stops the process. Also, the receiver must ask questions and clarify areas that are not clearly understood.

This material is only for "individual" spiritual growth. No two souls are identical. This material will either touch or not touch your soul. Each soul grows at its own pace and ability to understand. Each soul may interpret information totally differently, which is fine. Spiritual growth is not a one size fits all process. Each soul must experience and evolve at its own pace is the lesson repeated over and over. For this reason, those of us who have received information were advised that Creator does not approve of group discussions of the material. The danger is that—in a group—someone will try to convince others that his or her interpretation is most accurate. The information from Creator is for each soul to hear and respond as he or she is led to respond. This is the free will of each soul. This goes back to the quote given by Elijah for the first book: "Seek ye to know that which is true and having found It, hide it within thine own heart."

Throughout the years, the primary themes of channeled information have been: Creator made all that is. Creator is in charge of the heavens and the Earth. Jamiah is a humble servant of the Creator. Jamiah brings messages from Creator and Jamiah reports back to Creator. Creator knows all that is given to Earth and to individuals on Earth. Creator made each soul. He knows why he made each soul, what each soul chose as its purpose and its gifts, and how these gifts would be used to fulfill the soul's purpose.

Creator created all souls and never disconnected from any of them. Each soul created still has that spark that came from Creator—the original soul cell containing Creator's DNA and cell memory. Regardless of the number of lives lived and where they were lived—Earth, Mars, or elsewhere—the soul remains connected to the Creator through DNA and cell memory. More will be given on this process in later chapters.

The Creator has a Council or Councils that oversees the Earth life each soul is living. On Earth, spirit guides and guardian angels and others are assigned to assist and watch over each soul of light. Creator and our God of Earth give the final approval for the plan of the soul that is to enter Earth. The guides have access to the soul's chart in the Hall of Records. Creator has access, not only to those, but also others. He knows the minute details of our souls. The primary role of the guide is to keep the assigned human on its chosen path. The nudge of the conscience is actually the spirit guide reminding us.

Over the years, the information received has been of ever increasing depth. It began with *Heroes Without Halos* and continued with *Awakening of the Soul*. Now, finally, *Beyond Cell Memory* explains how human souls and forms containing souls on other planetary systems are connected to the Creator and how we are all one. Among the major topics brought forth are: how the physical cell was created and how the human physical form evolved; how Creator made the soul and when the soul enters the physical form. Also covered in detail are: how cell memory operates, how to clear traumatic cell memories on Earth, and how DNA and cell memory operate at death and thereafter. Other important topics included in *Beyond Cell Memory* are: abortions, homosexuality, organ transplants and transfer of cell memories through organ transplants.

Possible solutions to many of our human problems involve understanding DNA and cell memory. Those who work with DNA and cell memory must clearly understand the depth of what it is—its origin.

Now, it is important to know that the material in this book and the material in *Awakening of the Soul* were channeled at the same time, in the same sessions. At each of those sessions, the book that was to contain specific material was specified: this is for Awakening of the Soul; this is for the Cell Memory book. Therefore, some of the material was channeled in 2007 and 2008. This is especially true of the dream work with Dr. Freud.

Other material was channeled in 2011. For example, when I started to write about cell memory, I was not sure how to begin. Then Jamiah brought material from Creator that was clearly intended for the beginning of **Part I.**

In Part II, material channeled at earlier dates is presented. This material came from Edgar Cayce, Isaac Newton, Galilei Galileo, Sigmund Freud, and others. Now, how does the work of these men fit in with cell memory?

They came in support of this mission to get this channeled material to the public. They came to verify or validate that the information channeled is accurate information. They came to support and assist in completion of the project. These men, when they lived on Earth, looked to the *Beyond* in search of answers. They knew there was more to this Earth life than what they were taught or asked to believe. They saw more before their eyes in nature. They felt driven to learn, and they were independent thinkers, and they adhered to their convictions.

They saw connections and relationships and asked questions. They searched wherever they were led for answers. Some were led to the Bible, and historical literature, some developed tools such as telescopes, and microscopes, and scientific methods of study. The "scientific method" was deemed wrong or in conflict with the Catholic Church, and at times, others. At some point, many of these gifted souls with unusual ideas were challenged by the their peers, by church leaders, or other leaders.

So after hundreds of years, why are they channeling from the Beyond now? The answer is this: While they were on Earth, each one of them knew *inside* that there was more "out there," in the Beyond, than what they saw day-to-day. They knew there had to be a higher Source, a higher intelligence that created all that exists. From the Other Side, as we call it or heaven, they now confirm that the connection they sought is cell memory. DNA and cell memory exist in all that is—this includes all the universes, all the galaxies, and all the planetary systems, all the Gods over each planetary system, and each inhabitant of each planet of the planetary systems. This includes each of us. The DNA and cell memory are the threads that runs through all the material and connects all of us. Channeling to Earth now, is part of the reward to those who were diligent and worked so hard. An example of this is that Edgar Cayce's previous predictions that are occurring now. His error was timing. When he was on Earth, he did not know that Earth is the only place with time and religion.

Other special issues in this section are homosexuality, abortions, suicide, and transplants. The common thread in these topics is also DNA and cell memory.

In Part III, Creator sent Makala, who reports to Mother God, to explain Creator's energy and how the different densities of energy he created support and report back to Him. Her appearance set the stage for completion of this ten-year mission.

Part I

Origin, Purpose and
Use of DNA and Cell Memory

The overall message for this section is Creator made each soul with a cell of His/Her own energy. That cell contains an exact copy of His/Her DNA and cell memory. This is how we remain connected for all eternity. This is how all souls in all universes were created and this is how we are all connected. This is how Creator keeps track of where we are, what we are thinking, doing, and feeling. The connection is eternal. Creator is the highest of high.

These messages are given repeatedly in different words by different souls. There is a reason given for he repetition. It is like the advertisements on Earth. The more you hear the words and, in your mind, see the images that the words create, the more likely you are to remember the product. In this case, the product is our souls. He wants us to know and understand: how we were created, how we are carefully prepared to enter and exit earth, why we come to Earth, and what happens when we leave Earth. Creator has messages repeated in simple words so the average person may read and understand the truth about our souls and how we were created.

The information messengers brought are answers to questions humans have asked throughout our history. Even now, as sophisticated as we think we are, other civilizations have existed that were our equals or higher. And yes, there are souls living in different forms on other planets. Their physical forms, like ours, were created so that they could survive and sustain themselves in the specific environment of the given planet.

The messages make it clear that once souls were made they flitted about but, eventually, they wanted a suitable physical form to live in.

Creator pulled the best scientists from other planetary systems to design a form suitable for our souls of Earth to live in. He wanted a form that could reproduce and sustain itself. Once such a form was complete, souls entered the forms and began to stay in the forms for varying periods. At this point, souls knew how to speak directly with Creator and how to go back and forth from the physical form to the Other Side. Also, they communicated by telepathy; each knew the thoughts of the other. This was honesty.

With assistance from advanced planetary systems, our intelligence increased and, over time, we evolved to the present stage. Along with the intelligence also came problems but humans persevered and evolved to the point we have reached today.

Since Earth is currently the school of learning and the planet we occupy, the messages are geared for our understanding. Said another way, Messages are simplified for our understanding and level of intelligence while we occupy Earth. Our primary purpose for coming to Earth is to grow spiritually. While on the other side, we were prepared extensively for what to expect on Earth, and we were assigned spirit guides and others to support us and try to keep us on the path we chose. Once on Earth, we do not recall what we charted because we could not possibly function if all our lives were recalled. The veil we read about in the Bible prevents us from recalling our prior lives.

That veil is composed of time and religion. The veil drops with our first breath of life in (inspiration). The veil opens with our last breath of life out (expiration). When the veil opens, then we have access to the knowledge of the Other Side and our records since our soul was created. Now, a few special souls on Earth have *the true gift of prophecy* at this time. For these souls, the veil to the other side did not close completely at birth. They can still access certain records. This is what has been given and Naomi has such a gift.

1

Jamiah: Creator—DNA and Cell Memory

Who is Jamiah? Jamiah describes himself as the humble servant of Creator. Jamiah is a male energy. As he approaches Naomi, she describes his energy as very bright light that fills the whole room. Jamiah is a very high-energy that was made by Creator and he chose to remain near Creator. He has never been on Earth and speaks another language. He does not know our language well. Machines are available to convert his language to ours but he is stubborn and refuses to use them. Therefore, his speech pattern is often confusing and hard to understand and type. Since he does not know our language well he will say things like, "Jamiah come today."

Jamiah is also compassionate. On at least three occasions, he healed me of an illness. How did he do this? He instructed Naomi to place the palm of her hands flat on the souls of my feet. He said he pulled the energy out of my body that was making me ill. He said Creator told him to heal me so he follows the requests of Creator.

Jamiah is very protective of his position of service to Creator. Those who seek appointments with Creator are supposed to go through Jamiah. If souls do not comply, Jamiah gets upset. One soul in particular irks him. That soul is Elijah, the late marine/policeman. Jamiah refers to him as an annoyance "buzzing around his feet" and often reports him to Creator. They're a real comedy team, which Creator is said to find entertaining.

Also, I recall that those who crossed on 9/11/2001 were very cautious not to offend Jamiah. He apparently was in charge of their orientation and training once their souls were cleansed, debriefed and released from the processing area for new arrivals.

Now however, Elijah has adjusted to living as a soul on the Other Side. He has found ways to work around Jamiah and go to Creator. For one thing, he got promoted and may now report directly to Creator. His energy is different from that of Jamiah. He does not like waiting in line and such. He is more of a "giddy-up, get-it-done" type personality. Jamiah and Elijah together are almost like siblings that compete for attention. Jamiah is trying to learn English and how to be funny like Elijah. Once, at a gathering of about 15 females, Jamiah came through trying to speak like John Wayne and cowboys. He entered trying to sing and said: Howdy partners, I've been watching your television and learning to speak English. Everyone laughed and said, "he watched Westerns." Jamiah loved that he made us laugh. So, that is a glimpse at Jamiah. Now, let us get to his channeling.

On May 21, 2010, I went for my weekly reflexology treatment. As usual, I expected to also receive channeled material. I hoped that that I would be given assistance on how to relay the cell memory information to the public. I have page after page of information but I felt that I needed more specific information from experts in the field.

I was amazed at what happened. As if hearing my thoughts, Jamiah, who takes direct orders from Creator, appeared and spoke through the channel, Naomi. Since Jamiah's English is broken, I have filled in the verbs, which he usually omits. I have left his thoughts intact as received.

Jamiah

Jamiah is very happy today because Jamiah gets to see pretty lady. Creator said to me, Jamiah, you need to go now and talk to the pretty lady, the one who writes the books. What you need to say to her will come to you. You need to speak about the beginning of Earth and how it was in the beginning. I will give you this knowledge. I thought and thought about what Creator wants me to say. I know what Creator wants but I don't know how to say it. It is about the book you are to write. Oh, and I must say this to you: Creator loves the way you do other books. He would be angry with me if I forgot to say this.

I thanked Jamiah and said that I did not think Creator would be angry with him. Jamiah disagreed. He said, Creator does have the emotion of anger and he would be angry if he forgot. If he says do something, then I need to do it.

I have important news from the Creator about cell memory that he wants me to give to you. This comes directly from the Creator. The information is from the Creator. Creator hears all and knows all. Creator knows your conversations. He listens. I do not listen.

Creator has DNA and cell memory. Creator is the highest of energy, higher than anyone could imagine or that I can describe. Creator made each and every soul and with each one that he made, he began with one of his own cells. So, all souls that were made have DNA and cell memory from Creator. There are large numbers of souls that were made and each one has its own unique DNA and cell memory.

This same cell memory and DNA stay with the same soul forever. No matter where the soul goes the DNA and cell memory go too. The cell memory stay from the moment the Creator makes the soul. They are called strands of DNA. Creator wants me to tell you that each soul carries with it always—wherever it goes or whatever universe it goes to—DNA and cell memory. This is highly important information.

Creator is really excited about your book. It will show in writing what he means, how he did this, how he made this. Understand?

I answered yes, I understand. You said that in the beginning of creating a soul, Creator began with one cell. He took the cell from himself. In other words, when Creator made a soul, the cell he used to make each soul came from Himself/Herself. Therefore, each soul made by Creator has DNA and cell memory from Creator. Did I state it right?

Jamiah answered: That is right. Each soul made was from Creator. Each soul has DNA and cell memory from Creator. If each soul was made from Creator, then each soul has DNA and cell memory. What does that mean to you? It means—that in your book—you state it however you wish. Creator has cell memory stronger than all souls and DNA stronger than all souls.

If Creator—in making trillions of souls—used one of His cells containing DNA and cell memory for each soul, then that one cell

5

with DNA and cell memory is weaker than the Creator. It has to be. The DNA and cell memory of Creator is stronger than all those he made.

Creator said it is important that your book explain that no matter how many places a soul goes or how many lifetimes a soul has, the DNA and cell memory stay the same. You know this. Not all people know this but you know.

I responded that I had thought of this earlier in the week. Jamiah disagreed. Jamiah said: No, you did not think of this. Your Spirit Guide, Athena, gave you the thought, same difference.

This is highly complex. Each soul being different is very complex: different DNA, different cell memory, different throughout. But, in each life, the soul has the same markings. This is very complicated but simple. It is simple to the Creator.

Okay, I, Jamiah, will tell you what Creator means. On Earth now, scientists make an artificial baby in a laboratory. It does not have DNA and does not have cell memory that Creator makes. That is how you know if the soul is of God. You smart lady and know this already.

I, Grace, will restate my understanding. That cell made in the laboratory by scientists on Earth was not made by Creator. Creator didn't make that cell, so that cell has no soul because Creator did not make it. Is that correct?

That is correct Grace. This "soul," that man makes, thinks as human.

So Jamiah, let me state it this way. This being is not connected to Creator. This being created in the laboratory has no soul from Creator. Creator did not make the being. Is this correct?

Very good Grace, this being is not connected to Creator. Creator does not claim this being because to have a soul, it must come from Creator. That does not mean the baby can't function. It can function but not with a soul from Creator.

I have a question, Jamiah. Are these beings more like robots? Jamiah answered, they function and appear as human but have no feeling—more like robots—they do not have feelings as humans that Creator makes. This is very difficult for me to explain. Creator put a lot on Jamiah.

Creator has more that I, Jamiah, must give to you. *Creator wants you to explain in the book that it is very easy for Him to keep up with souls.* He has a special way and place where he keeps records. The method Creator uses is similar to how you on Earth track people. The device Creator has keeps the identity of each soul the Creator made. Wherever the soul goes, Creator knows and records this. If the soul is in a universe over here or here or there, Creator looks at where the soul was made and a special signal comes from the soul, so Creator knows where the soul is. *That is how Creator knows and hears prayers from humans or creatures from other planetary systems.* A prayer lights up the system. It is a light-up system—bing, bing. It is the same as the system you have on Earth for tracking a vehicle or human.

Now you know of this. I have told you this so that you would understand. It is not complex like many on your planet think. Many people on Earth think they are the only race, the only souls. There are many universes and many planets and all have souls. Planets are within universes and planets have souls.

Creator is more magnificent than humans know. Creator is not limited in just soul making. Creator also made universes and planets. Each planet has a soul, a soul that is different from humans. Creator is magnificent, a word that Jamiah likes. Magnificent—greater than, more than—I cannot describe or put into words what Creator is. Now, back to what Creator wants me to do, tell you about the cell memory book.

Be sure to write this in the book. Each soul—on the journey it takes—carries with it the cell memory of previous lives—wherever it may have been for a reason. You see, when your soul goes back to the Other Side, your soul clears all negatives by going through the chambers. The one that channels calls this debriefing. *The Chamber is where one clears all negatives. All scenes that were not good are erased. Cell memory of the good, the beneficial, is retained for encouragement of the soul in the next life on a planet.*

Cell memory of the negative or the not nice things may be retained if the soul desires to work on clearing these in another incarnation. The soul may choose to do this. Creator allows this. This is where karma comes in. In this case, the cell memory of the good and the chosen negative would be retained and taken to the next incarnation. Earth is a school of learning. Clearing karmas is another way of going back to Creator faster.

You two chose coming here to assist other souls. By electing to come here to assist others, you are faster at going back to Creator. Your works exemplify—you help others. You aid others. There are many stages of development of the soul. The one I speak through says kindergarten and so on, like your schools do. This is a good way to explain this. This is a good way because a soul down here on Earth is just beginning to learn lessons by experience. I am trying hard to do exactly what Creator wants me to do so that I don't have to repeat the lesson. Jamiah knows that what Creator wants written in the books is important.

The action of each soul is determined by that soul. Creator makes souls. Souls are carefully prepared to go out into the universe. The soul makes a choice of what to say, what to do and what acts it will commit. Souls are on their own in these choices. Creator has training for each soul. Each soul has the choice to act or not act, as it was trained or prepared to act.

We do not send you, your soul, out in the universe without knowing what is good and what is bad. You also have within your DNA and cell structure, the ability to know Dark Energy. Creator placed this in your DNA—so that when you come upon Dark Energy—you withdraw, you stay away. Each soul makes a choice of action. Each soul may choose to protect itself and stay away from Dark Energy or the soul may be persuaded by Dark Energy to do wrong. That decision is up to the soul.

DNA and cell memory have a program, as a computer has a program. Creator placed this program there to give warnings of Dark Energy. The warnings of Dark Energy and their influence of wrong action are day-by-day—continuously—you have a program there. Many call this conscience—consciousness—that they think with, that is in the brain of a human. On other planetary systems, they have other ways of detecting Dark Energy. This is very complex to explain so Jamiah will stay with the Earth that you are familiar with.

This is so hard to get through. You are very smart pretty lady, but Jamiah has a hard time giving you what Creator wants. The main lesson for you to know and explain is that each soul made by Creator has DNA and cell memory. Each human has a program within the brain area that allows him or her to a make right or wrong choice. If, on Earth, you make a wrong choice your soul goes through a clearing process. Your soul retains DNA and cell memory. Also, if you choose during the clearing, you may keep cell memory of actions that hurt others and work on correcting those actions in a future life. In that case, it is up to each soul to place itself where others they hurt are located so they can make amends for wrong acts or harmful deeds.

That is what you on Earth call karma. We call it poor judgment. Other planetary systems call it other things. Creator placed the program within all souls. So all souls use the same program no matter where they are located.

Vast, vast are the universes and the majority of souls make progress by coming to Earth. It is a school, as Creator designed. Souls that come to Earth have the opportunity to grow faster and come back to Creator. On Earth, souls learn of emotions—love, caring, compassion and acceptance. Also, souls learn of negative emotions. They learn how to deal with them and how to avoid the negative, the Dark Energy.

Other universes do not have as much growth because there is not as much to work with and there are fewer souls there to work with anything. You may go to other planetary systems and they allow other means of learning. Earth gives you the opportunity to grow in soul and go back home.

Now, Creator says, "Ask and you shall receive." Jamiah feels that he said too much in one day. Jamiah's energy is strong but is now depleted. You understand and are very smart in all you do. You've had training in many planetary systems. Abilities in you are tremendous.

Jamiah states a fact. Jamiah loves working with you. Creator said Jamiah, make information simple so others that read information in book know what it means. Jamiah tried to stay simple.

I thanked Jamiah and then said to him, I have written statements for my book. I want you to tell me if they are accurate. The statements are: Creator made all planets. Creator made all souls. Earth is the school of learning for all souls. Before coming to Earth, each soul must develop a detailed plan or chart for what he or she is to experience/learn on Earth. This plan is presented to committees and finally to the Council. The Council, God of Earth, and Creator must give final approval of this soul's plan to come to Earth. If approved, the soul—using the information in this chart—is assisted in a process called soul regression, while on the Other Side. This helps prepare the soul for what it will experience when it comes to Earth.

My mother Emma described the process of soul regression in my book, *Awakening of the Soul*. She gave an overview of how each soul is regressed to the fetal stage. She was among those trained to assist the souls preparing to enter the Earth. She worked with those who had already regressed to the infant stage. This stage required more intense care by other souls, just like on Earth, infants require much care. (Grace J. Scott 2009)

In this process, souls—in what we call heaven—appear a certain chosen age, usually about thirty. They are regressed in stages from that age all the way back to infancy. During each stage—say age thirty to age twenty, the soul feels and reviews what it will experience. The purpose of this is to prepare that soul coming onto earth. This preparation lets the soul know what to expect all the way from birth on Earth forward through its lifespan on Earth. Do you follow me, Jamiah?

Yes, Jamiah understands. You are correct, except Jamiah adds: They know but it is hidden so they may experience.

As I, Grace, understand it, this information is hidden when we are born. It is hidden by the veil created here—linear time and religion. I was told previously that man, not God, created time and religion. The whole thing sounds confusing to me.

Jamiah answered that it is correct that time and religion are obstacles on Earth. But he explained and corrected my perception: Time and religion were "not introduced" into us, they were "not placed within us" before we came to Earth. The soul was "informed of the obstacles of linear time and religion so that the soul could be aware that the soul does not need these." The soul is informed by the Council before coming to Earth so the soul knows what to expect. However, once the soul is on planet Earth (in the human form) it forgets all that was stated, but inside (the human) the soul knows. Some people do recall and have information come to the surface. "These stay away from religion or attend briefly and pull back."

Now the Council is located outside the planet Earth. (I verified that this area is what we call heaven). Also, Jamiah said that each planet has such an area outside of it that serves a similar purpose—preparing souls that leave and clearing souls that reenter their area. (This process has been compared to our passport system.). Before each soul comes to Earth that soul makes a chart of what the soul is to experience and learn because Earth is a school of learning for all souls from all planetary systems. As souls are preparing to come to Earth, the soul must present the planned chart to the Council for approval. This is a very big process. Members of the Council committees carefully work with each soul and help each one prepare to come to Earth.

Jamiah spoke of Dark Energies or how souls get off their charted paths. For simplicity, I will restate what Jamiah said. When Creator made souls and gave them his DNA and cell memory, he also gave them free will. As souls entered humans on Earth, and as humans reincarnated on Earth, they grew in intellect. As this happened, "some souls saw the opportunity for money. Religion was created for the purpose of money—to control humans and get money. Both money and control

11

are tools of evil or dark energy. Creator never programmed or stated to souls to worship in a building or to worship in a form or to control individuals."

Jamiah continued that: The "Dark Energy does not have these obstacles of time and religion. They honor time. They do not honor religion. They attend religious groups or places of religion to create problems. Dark energies know what causes problems. Dark Energy is in all religions. They do not go before the Council. They do not get assistance from the Council.

There are good humans in churches. The problems are the leaders and control. In the beginning, your book the Bible shows Moses and others leading people under God's direction. No talk of priests and ministers. Early people turned to Creator, called upon God, called upon Son, or whatever name they called Creator, for direction.

Everything went wrong when head of this group of people decided it was time to worship a name, worship a human, worship a priest, worship a rabbi, and place them there proclaiming to be of God, claiming to be religion. That is when it got off track.

The ones that want no fame, no popularity with other peoples, they are of God. It got bad when the Dark Energy said, now we will go in and make more money and make more troubles and we tell people what to do. Give us money and pay off your sins. Give us money and build bigger church. Give us money and we will help this person. Money is evil. Barter is better. Glad you asked, pretty lady.

Jamiah will now go back to Creator. Hope pretty lady is okay with what Jamiah said. I gave a little at time so people will understand. More cases will be placed in your path. The book must get out it is very important." End

2

Oshinbah: Creation and Evolution of Life on Earth

Oshinbah is what we would call an ambassador. He travels among the various universes, galaxies and planetary systems and reports his findings to Creator. The first time he appeared to Naomi she gave this description of him: He is tall and has a head that is much larger than ours. His ears are also larger and stand out from his head. He appears to have very kind eyes, tiny holes for a nose and a tiny mouth. His uniform is a silver tight fitting suit. At another time, she said he reminded her of the Jolly Green Giant because of his size and he had no hair on his head or face.

Oshinbah says that his planetary system residents are of a much higher intelligence than residents of Earth. He always comes in peace and to help us. He informed us that his planet of origin is Venus, although he travels a lot. For communication, he does use the machine that converts his language to ours. Sometimes, there is static but it's usually clear. Like Jamiah, he often starts a sentence with his own name.

Now Oshinbah wanted his description given to us because eventually we will see residents of other planets. Other planetary systems, by request of Creator, are surrounding and assisting the Earth because of the upcoming changes. Changes on our planet impact other planetary systems. Some of these souls assist souls of light to their new home when they leave Earth. They also assist Earth by escorting dark energies to assigned areas. The dark and the light never mix on the Other Side.

Oshinbah informed us that he and others like him are able to change their appearance and attire at will. When they appear to Naomi or should they appear to one of us, they would look like us so that we would not be frightened.

Over the last several years, the entity known as Oshinbah has been very informative and helpful. In addition, Elijah is now his assistant.

Together, they will be working diligently with the Earth changes on their side and preparing us to cope on this side.

Today is 5/28/2010. I told Naomi about my session last weeks and some of the thoughts I've had since. Then Oshinbah came to channel through Naomi. He commented that his English is broken because he must slow his energy vibrational level to match that of Naomi.

Oshinbah

Oshinbah is delighted to come again. I have not been here in quite a time, Earth time. You are aware that Elijah and I work together. Elijah is easy for me to work with. Many others do not think so. Elijah is of very, very high energy and he accomplishes more than others in smaller amount of Earth time. Elijah is very valuable. But, Oshinbah did not come to talk about Elijah.

Jamiah was here last week and he reported back to Creator. Creator informed Oshinbah that he must come and speak some information that Creator wishes for you to have. It may be connected to your cell memory work. Since Oshinbah travels all universes and all the different areas that Creator created, Creator informed me to give you descriptive information of the occurrences around earth and also, information pertaining to Earth.

Oshinbah has enough information to speak from now until Earth changes. However, I have been informed of what information that I am to give to you, dear lady. The information is not only for you but for all who read your books. Creator wishes the information be placed in the book for all to read. The information I have is connected with how the Earth began, its origin. I'm not going to do a boring history.

The misconception on Earth about Creator and Earth is that the planet Earth had been used as an experiment. This is what we call a myth. Planet Earth was not used as an experimental station as many think that it was.

This is correct information: Creator created the Earth and when Earth was completed, it had all the elements necessary to support life but it was barren. Creator wished the beginning of an energy mass that would become human in form. The life form and the elements available on the planet had to be suitable, useful, and compatible with each other.

To develop this life form and see what would live on Earth, Creator selected the best scientists, as you understand the word. They were brought to Earth from the higher developed races of the higher developed universes. He selected and brought to Earth the most highly developed scientists. These scientists were of professions that knew how to begin cells. Cells are the beginning of life. So, those of the higher intellect—collectively, from other planetary systems, other universes—arrived on Earth at the request of Creator.

The scientists arrived on Earth by a means of travel that is not known on Earth at present. In other words, they traveled from planetary systems that are not within reach by Earth technology, even now. Travel was done by space ships more modern than you of Earth have even dreamed of or made sketches of and we still have these.

We speak to you by thought. The space ships travel in a similar way. They travel by thought from the planetary systems very far from Earth. You have been given information that when you leave Earth and go to the Other Side, you create things by thought. Whatever you wish to have, you think it and it becomes or materializes. This is similar to how they arrived on Earth.

Let me explain: If you have ever had the privilege of watching certain *Star Trek* movies, in the movies they say, "Beam me up." Then all cells disintegrate and then reenergize or reassemble in a new location. This is very similar to how a spaceship with scientists onboard arrived on Earth. All of the scientists here study and know how to do this.

These advanced, intelligent, informed beings came to Earth and that is how they arrived. This is highly important for individuals to know because your scientists of high intellect on Earth will eventually learn to travel by this means. They will learn how human cells disintegrate intact and reenergize or regroup intact in another place far away. *The cell is connected.* However, I must stick to the message Creator told me to bring.

When the scientist and those of high intellect arrived on Earth, they already had with them the means of restructuring cells that they knew could only grow on Earth. Many planets have life, but not as Earth life. The composition of Earth elements and of human elements, have to match. Earth elements—oxygen, hydrogen, and all of these components—you need to be chemistry person to know all this. Anyway, they began that process. The first cell structure was a very simple form. They began, not in a dish as your scientists do, but just in a space here on Earth.

Because of the advanced knowledge of these scientists, life began on all "places" of Earth. In other words, it was not limited to a certain continent. These beings that came to Earth for this purpose scattered throughout. There was no such thing on other planetary systems as color or race or however you wish to present it. It is soul. Now, as a creative measure—no matter what your books or your Bible state, the colors or races began with these original scientists that were the workers in this field. These scientists were positioned on the landmasses that you now call continents. Each team originated the cells that would grow into humans on their continent.

As advanced as scientists are at this time on Earth, it is not their original thought to begin an artificial being in a dish. This began when scientists came on Earth and there was no life whatsoever. This is why Creator over God and God over Earth decided to have teams on each continent. As these teams made progress in the development of humans, they began with the animals and with the fish—with that of the ocean. It was an experiment at that time—to see if they could perfect what you now call human. I could spend perhaps a year talking and go back to the original cell being developed. However, that is not what Creator said to do.

Briefly this is what happened: first, these high intellect beings developed reptiles and underwater species. Then they developed a more advanced species that would have the ability to control its own environment, have a longer life, and would be able to reproduce in a means by touching—by intercourse—enter, to go within. The animals and reptiles would reproduce by similar means but their reproductive action would be by instinct. The primary species (that is human beings) were more intelligent and not only could control their own environment; they were able to dominate the lower species as a food chain. This arrangement is still in place on Earth. It was not an experiment subject to later evaluation. It was the fulfillment of a deliberate, planned design.

Now, this is the way the color or what you call races occurred. Each scientific group placed on each continent realized they had to create a human form that could live in the particular type of climate and environment of that continent. If it was one of extreme heat that had developed, then the human placed there had to be one that could live in this extreme heat. In doing this, the dark skin was more acclimated for the moisture, heat and sun than the light skin. Therefore, the scientists of each continent that developed their own species of human also developed the different skin tones to accommodate where the humans lived. That was the purpose, not what the book of the Bible states. It is not as though those of the scientific field were experimenting. They knew that to accomplish what they had come to achieve, they needed a human race that could live in a certain environment.

They had to have a human form that could adapt to that particular area, that particular region or continent. As time progressed, (humans developed) chemicals and the chemical related products that could cover the skin so all could integrate. Then the modern methods of travel occurred and you began the integration of all races that you have at the present time. I, Oshinbah, was told to inform you of this and then move on to other subjects. That one is covered.

Creator wishes you to know that—because of the importance of Earth and Creator sending those of highest of all intellect to Earth—Creator also now protects Earth until the planet expires. What Creator and scientists did not do—and Creator knows how to do but did not inform or instruct—was the means of preventing dark energy from coming onto Earth.

Dark Energy began invading when human life became more perfected. This gave them the opportunity to inhabit the physical. They could grow on their level, the Dark Energy level, from what was zero to a number of three of the development. Planet Earth would allow this because they would inhabit human bodies.

Creator created the dark energy; he made it as light energy but the energy itself refused to be of Creator. So Creator allowed the energy to divert and go its own way. At the time, very few were Dark Energy. They began on Earth to take on human form and multiply into more Dark Energy. Plus, Dark Energy also persuaded many of the Light Energy to cross over into dark. This was not pleasing to Creator. Dark Energy is very destructive. Dark Energy entered planet Earth and became destructive with Earth itself. The Dark Energy also invaded all that was good. And Dark Energy began making the bad, the negative. Where you are now, you are very aware that planet Earth is very limited on time. The changes to occur on Earth are imminent. However, a regimen of the best of protectors from the universes—what you would call military—are and have been surrounding Earth. I am skipping, with permission of Creator, the "in-between"—the beginning of all this, and going to where you are now.

The Dark Energy so invaded the Earth that it has almost consumed it. In the invading and consuming of Earth, the destructive forces of chemicals have been opened on the Earth's surface. And the planet itself, the energy of the planet is expiring. That is what is creating the destructive nature of Earth. Obviously, you do not have to be of high intellect to know that as Dark Energy souls destroyed Earth, they have also destroyed their own home. They will go elsewhere and find a planetary system.

Creator wished that you know all of this because cell energy is highly important and DNA is highly important. The next planetary system that human life lives on will be planet Venus. Even those of the highest intellect have learned from this. Planet Venus will be constructed or embellished or surrounded with a means of repelling the Dark Energy. Some Dark Energy can possibly invade but not as it has on Earth.

Those human beings—the spirits in human form now on Earth—and those that have crossed over—if they so desire, they may take on the human form again on the planet Venus. But they will not be subjected to Dark Energy. There will be preventive measures taken by those of the military forces that occupy around planet Earth, at this time. They will establish a center around the planet Venus. They have much more modern equipment than I can even describe. I know what the equipment is but I am not permitted to give the information. However, you can envision it as a net with reverse mirrors surrounding the Earth and throwing the Dark Energy back into an empty space.

This is overwhelming information. I have had to eliminate a lot of information that would have given more explanations. I am trying to condense what Creator wanted given so that I will not confuse anyone. At the same time, I am trying to give information that will be beneficial.

The purpose of the Creator having me do this is so you will be more enlightened about missions on planet Venus. Also, be enlightened, all of you on Earth, that after the Earth changes, you will not have dark energy on Earth. This has been spoken of before.

Oshinbah is here today to let you know that the vibrational level after the Earth changes will be so strong that all humans who remain on Earth will have direct communication with other planetary systems. In other words, the energy of all who remain will be high enough to communicate with all planetary systems. At that time, it will no longer be necessary for any to channel through a gifted person, as I am now doing to reach you.

As has been given before to you, you will not die. The physical you will not expire. You will just transport. Many that inhabit Earth after the change will elect to go directly to Venus. They know, their souls knows, what is there waiting for them. After the changes, the environment of Venus will be similar to that of Earth—meaning of pure energy and direct connection with Creator on the planet Venus.

The other universes throughout the planetary systems are still growing. There are planetary systems that allow you to come in forms other than human. But the return to Creator is at a slower rate than the school of learning planet.

Therefore, those who are of the higher energy (as the two of you are) that remain on Earth and continue the escalation of higher energy will be ideal candidates for planet Venus as it begins its operation. You will be as the outer space people or as other planetary systems were with the planet Earth. (You could opt to go to Venus but you two will not elect to do so). Those who do remain and do elect to go to Venus will be the pioneers in establishing a life form on the planet of Venus.

Now, this is what Creator wished for you to have. Why? I do not know. I came as instructed and gave you this information. I am positive of one thing. Creator never instructs Oshinbah to come forth and divulge information unless Creator has a definite purpose. This purpose may be revealed by Jamiah, Oshinbah or Elijah—all are higher energy souls. I am today carrying out instructions from Creator.

I said to Oshinbah, the human form that the soul lives in—is the human form the highest of functioning forms?

Oshinbah replied: No. The human form that you occupy was one that developed, as I stated, by those who came here on a special mission. They designed the form. As you are aware on earth of designers of clothing, each one has his or her thoughts of the design process, so it was with the human body being developed.

I said to Oshinbah, I need clarification on this: In the Bible, the book we have here, it says that man was made in the image of the Creator. I think what I am trying to do is absorb—in my mind what you just said—and then take the soul, made by Creator—and place it in this human form or in this context.

Oshinbah said: To give you correct information, I, Oshinbah tell you—when words speak "made in the image"—this refers to soul. Soul was made in the image of Creator, not form, not physical. There are many different forms on different planets, different systems.

I said, let me see if I have this right. Creator made each soul, and all souls. All souls were made in the image of the Creator. All souls made by Creator have DNA and cell memory. All souls may live in different forms and all souls may live on different planets in different planetary systems. Is that right? Oshinbah said yes.

I then stated the information I have been given is that when Creator made anything, regardless of what, he started with one cell. And the one cell multiplied. But, the one cell originally came from the Creator—like he took one cell from self—His/Her energy. Right?

Oshinbah said: You are very smart and you know but much of what you know comes because you are of higher energy. Now, many are of intellect, but you know because you recall from Creator the creation—of soul—of you.

Okay, Oshinbah will explain it. On Earth you have a container called "shoebox." Shoebox contains a different item inside, which can be different each time the box is opened. Planets are the same way. Inside is a different form for soul to occupy. Is that okay? Do you understand?

I answered yes. This is my understanding. Creator made each planet for a specific purpose. Each planet has certain elements. For anything to live on a planet, it must have the same elements as the planet provides. The life form must be compatible with the planet. In that sense, they help sustain each other. Creator and God of that planet must give final approval of the life form that a soul will occupy. Creator makes all souls starting with a cell of his own energy, his own DNA and cell memory. That is my understanding. And now, as usual, I have another question.

I have been told that there are two different strands of DNA that the Rainbow children now have. What are they and what do they do?

Oshinbah responded: The DNA strands of Rainbow children are as Creator created souls from the beginning, Creator used from self. Creator still, with Rainbow, used from self—more of core energy.

As Naomi spoke for Oshinbah, she placed her right hand on her heart area. She then moved her hand in a clockwise motion. Oshinbah said this movement by the one speaking is to illustrate the Creator's center. Creator took from His very heart, His core of energy—the DNA of the Rainbow Children. Rainbows have different strands of DNA. Just as material in the center of higher energy is different—that is how the DNA of a Rainbow child is different.

I said, from what I've read in books—the human cell has a nucleus—that is where the DNA and cell memory are located.

Oshinbah responded: *The cell nucleus of the human cell—this information has not been given before—the cell nucleus of the human cell is the same—exact duplicate of Creator's. You understand. I know you do because I felt it. I felt your energy change as I spoke.*

I now say to you, Creator does not play favoritism. And, we do not recognize time. But as eternity continued, then there was more of a requirement for a core of high energy so that all may be centered—all may return to centering. Rainbows have DNA strands for that purpose.

I said to Oshinbah—when we get to the "New Earth," will these new little children will be leaders—is that how this is connected?

Oshinbah answered: That is right. That is correct, but also, new planet—that of Venus—will continue on this path of a new DNA strand.

I asked if these Rainbows, these new little children, would be going to Venus to be leaders of Venus. Oshinbah said they have a choice of going to Venus or going back close to Creator. The reason for that is there are not as many with the extra DNA strands. Creator prefers fewer of these with extra DNA strands because their energy is so different—it would strain Creator's equilibrium—it would create an imbalance if too much DNA were taken from the center of self.

Oshinbah noticed that Lydia arrived for her appointment and said invite Lydia in. Lydia entered as requested. Oshinbah and Lydia greeted each other by saying namaste.

Oshinbah proceeded to address Lydia by saying: I spoke to these ladies this morning and I wish to acknowledge on behalf of Creator, your importance. Creator knew that you would come today, so I invite you all to stay and hear this. Creator knew that this one would be coming before Oshinbah had to leave. So, Creator wanted this message given to this one and others who have been affected by natural causes on Earth. (This reference is to the recent flood suffered by the state of Tennessee).

Creator wishes you to know that this flood was not a test. It was not a test. You grew from it. Creator knows your energy is high enough that when this challenge arrived in your life, all energy of humans affected went way down. Creator observed and knows that those that are of higher vibration come back fast. Also, Creator wishes you to know this, use this as an opportunity and develop higher energy from it. This is not why the accident or situation happened. The situation was of a natural cause. However, opportunity was given by the situation so that you might grow in spiritual high energy. You rose to the occasion. You grew from this.

This one (Grace) has all the information from Oshinbah on future events and what occurs now. However, if there is any other information that Oshinbah now gives, you may also have it.

Oshinbah does not have much longer to give information. I wish to now address the fact that those forces now surrounding Earth are not only for protective reasons—they will not interfere with what you call natural disasters—these will happen because Earth is weeping. Earth is not able to cleanse at this time. It is overpowered with chemicals and denseness. Earth's soul screams out in pain. Creator hears Earth's cry. Creator knows those of high vibration in connection with Creator desire for Earth to be cleansed.

Recent events of your area were not of the cleansing. This was because of negativity and Earth hitting or coming together. This was to make people aware and give them the opportunity to approach Creator, to call out and ask for help.

Oshinbah observed the whole process. Oshinbah understands why this area, your area, is safe when Earth begins change. All souls in this area that Oshinbah observed—this area, this state—was named for Indian occupant called Tennessee. An Indian occupant was called Tennessee. Tennessee occupants are of higher vibration. Many come into the area from other directions seeking that which Creator can give.

All of Earth is surrounded for protection of Earth and also, for protection of those who cross or choose to leave—as in the water condition your area had. Many chose to leave. Some chose a fun way to leave. Many humans who heard of this felt it was very foolish to get on raft or whatever you call these things. But souls thought it entertaining to leave in that method. Their choice, it was their choice. Families should not mourn these souls. They elected to leave so that they would be remembered in that way—they went out with bravery—they chose to explore. Those souls that left, it was planned before they came to Earth. The storm system itself was not planned to be so severe. However, the souls that left knew they would have this opportunity to leave in the floodwater.

Now, Creator, because of the incident, wishes all of you to know that much has been accomplished because of this. There will be a coming together of like souls. The coming together of like souls has already been done and there is much helping of others.

What Creator says to Oshinbah to give you all is this: The information is within you. The souls are awakening! Grace has written of this in her books.

The missions will be run smoothly when changes occur because of the cooperation of other planets—other planetary systems—willingly, freely, lovingly—sending forth their best of all units to assist with this.

The much-loved spirit, Elijah, will be leading all of this. One of the purposes of Elijah being over and assisting with all of the planetary systems is so that he may become familiar with all of the operations and those who are over all of the units that assist. Also, he must be familiar with all of the units trained to have empowerment over the Dark Energies. They are in good hands with Elijah. The Dark Energy will not interfere.

Oshinbah feels honored that Elijah assists with this. Oshinbah is free then to begin overseeing the operation on Venus. Also, Elijah assists with this! Elijah is a very important soul, as all souls are important to Creator.

Oshinbah has fulfilled the beginning elements that Creator requested. My heart leaped with joy, as you say on Earth, when Creator summoned and said: Go speak.

Jamiah was here last week and reported back to Creator. Creator acknowledged and recognized Jamiah. Creator requested that Oshinbah enlighten you about cell memory, beginning of Earth, and procedures—anyway—it was a brief lesson—let's say—about the beginning.

Oshinbah finds it very delightful to be with you and explain as much as allowed to explain. Much wonderful opportunities are coming forth for all—not in tragedies—what you call tragedies—we call enlightenment. Earth people forget on purpose. They could not begin their journeys if they had recall of other times or other journeys. Earth, as stated, is a school. This school is about to be let out for a definite or indefinite time. School system, as you know it, has advanced and has been perfected and will continue on the planet Venus. You may or may not have decided to journey to Venus and the next school system. If you did not, then you are going to higher learning journeys and Oshinbah will still see you no matter where you are.

You will recognize my energy. Do not forget that—after Earth changes—you will continue your journey. It will be high vibration for you and you can communicate directly with any of us. When you do leave Earth, before its final closing, you will just go. And that will not be death. Your soul will be free as a bird, as you say. You will take the wings of an eagle and go whatever destination you have chosen. For now, I bid to you a most fond farewell on behalf of Creator. Farewell is not a word of our language; it is one of yours on Earth. Over here we do Namaste. Blessings on all. End

3

Oshinbah and Celonious: Preparation and Selection

of Souls to Enter Earth

On June 18, 2010, I had my usual appointment with Naomi. She asked about my book. I told her how that I had tried writing in a different format. I read a few pages of how I wrote the new format. I hope someone will tell me today how I am to write this book—what style.

I read the words—that before the soul enters the Earth, the soul is taught on the Other Side about what to expect on Earth. Naomi said, that is very interesting but how can you incorporate that into cell memory? I answered: You are doing the same thing I did, at first. You have to think of the physical self and the soul separately.

Remember the soul was already made by Creator and already contains cell memory and DNA. The original, individual soul—with its cell memory and DNA of the Creator—exists eternally. Each soul is prepared—while on the Other Side—for what to expect from birth to whatever age it charted as the final opportunity to exit. (This was covered in my book *Awakening of the Soul.* Emma spoke of Soul Regression). We have the same soul for all eternity. The same soul has the same DNA and cell memory for many lives in many different bodies. We're all part of the Creator because he made us from His/Her energy. We are told this on the other side. We just don't remember. The soul containing DNA and cell memory of the Creator must enter the human form. The cell is the structure that contains the soul DNA and cell memory. It all goes back to Creator.

The human form, the human self is physically formed from cells. This physical shell is the house that was designed for the soul to enter and live in while on Earth. Like the robot mentioned before, the developing physical human baby in the uterus has DNA from the mother and the father. But until the new soul enters this fetus, it is just a batch of tissue.

27

I think that is how it works. Naomi said, until the soul made by Creator enters and becomes part of the baby, it is just tissue. Oh, someone has arrived to channel. It is Oshinbah.

Oshinbah: Introduction of Celonious

Oshinbah says: Oshinbah has arrived and desires to enter your world, into your magnificent human universe that has been explained in an excellent manner by the one who spoke. Souls that desire to come to Earth and grow spiritually must go before Councils and present their planned charts and get approval of the Councils, then God of your planet and Creator before entering Earth.

I bring with me today one who is a member of the Council that gives final approval of the soul before the birth on Earth. The individual's name is spelled Celonious. We do not go by rank but Celonious is the "Head Council Person" and has been since creation. You do not get promoted to this position, you are appointed by Creator. Celonious wished, upon hearing your review, *to give you more information.*

He wishes to give you his view or his perception of the training process of the soul. Before the soul arrives anywhere, not just Earth, it must be prepared. Primarily, Celonious will explain to you the steps, more of the details. Also, he wishes me to tell you that you may ask questions wherever you feel one is needed. This information will be incorporated into the cell memory book.

Also, I have information to share with you. However, Creator felt the appearance of Celonious overrode the information I was to give. This information will be given at a later date. To have the book proceed as you are writing it, you need the input from Celonious.

I also wish to give you this. I understand that you wished an opinion from Creator or those representing Creator about the format of the next book. The one you first read, when you went on a different angle, is the one Creator likes. It is the one that finds favor, not only with Creator, but also with Jamiah, myself and your best friend and buddy, Elijah. Elijah is exuberant about this and wishes to take credit for part of it. He informed Creator that he was persuasive of you when you were asleep. Maybe he did, but Creator does not care how it arrived just so that it arrives as he wishes. Elijah insists on being part of your life, even in the subconscious. You deal with this rather well. Creator finds it quite amusing and also, there is the ongoing verbal between Jamiah and Elijah. It is a comedy act for Creator. He does enjoy a comedy and these two make quite a comedy team. I have trouble when each of them speaks to me with their words, but that is fine, I am able to defend. Now, Celonious is going to speak with you. I will remain in the background.

Celonious

Celonious said: Celonious finds it interesting to speak. Celonious is awkward with this. This, my friends, is my first time to do this. Many have written books on Earth but none of this manner. Celonious was summoned by Creator and addressed by Creator to participate. Celonious must speak in this manner because of the newness of this situation. Also, I, Celonious do not speak the language of Earth.

Celonious wishes to inform you that information given already concerning the soul decreasing in age from thirty to child and baby is correct. There is not too much that I, Celonious, can add to your information except for the fact that there was a question about Dark Energy.

No Dark Energy is allowed in the process. Dark Energy only invades an unborn child, when parents—especially the mother has not put forth the desire of what the baby should be in the future. I speak of the personality of the baby, not the sex of the baby. The desire of the mother that the unborn baby is of God, of Creator, protects the baby from Dark Energy. When this desire is missing, the dark may easily enter the baby. All mothers-to-be should be given this information. *The parents, especially the mother, should express their desires for a child that is of God, of the Creator, for now and the future.*

The mothers should also be informed about when the soul enters the baby. Souls like freedom. Souls do not like confinement. Some souls do not

29

enter the baby until birth. Of those souls that enter the baby before birth, few have the soul enter the fetus earlier than the seventh or eighth month of the term. Souls will hover around the mother-to-be to experience and get accustomed to the voices of the mother and the family. It is better this way than inside the mother. But very few of the unborn have the soul enter earlier than the seventh or eighth month of the term.

Now, while on our side—as the soul decreases in age and as it approaches the approximate Earth age of six years—the soul from that point on does not recall life on our side. We have special guides that will be appointed to help this soul regress from Earth age six—on our side—until entering Earth. Those special guides do not go with this child to Earth. *One guide is selected and is known as the Spirit Guide for that individual soul.*

The soul has agreed to enter into the situation that it is entering into on Earth. In other words, the soul knows if the father is an alcoholic, or if the mother is a thief, or if the parents are highly religious. The purpose of the souls of parents on Earth was chosen before they went down to Earth. The soul that we send—elected to go into their world—(the purpose is) not of fulfilling Dark Energy, but of giving opportunity to parents to learn and come back on track. Now, much information was given to you on other aspects of this.

However, I, Celonious will give to you today, that a lot of screening is done for souls before they come onto Earth. *The Council screens very severely.* The soul may be selected and go through other screenings and be approved. But when the soul arrives before the Council, we may have turned back (not approved) that soul. We do not approve just because others have approved. We know more information about the situation on Earth. We know that—while man and woman were on this side, the soul (of the baby to be) elected to be with them—then the man and woman got to Earth and then their lives changed. Then the soul (baby) on this side is not obligated to go. The soul here does not know what we of the Council know. So the Council informs the soul that there is no longer a contract with these two because these two—mother and father—changed their path. Your going to them now would not aid them in the path they walk.

That happens sometimes. Another situation may be that this soul elected and contracted with an individual mother, no father. There is a purpose in that. People on Earth must understand that a baby may come to a mother and have no (legal) father. This helps the life purpose. It helps the body/soul purpose grow to what you call on Earth, karma. This soul of the baby enters a "one-parent life" on purpose. It helps create or fulfill the karma of mother. It helps that soul throughout life. The Council carefully chooses this soul.

As you are aware, all souls have five exits. We counsel souls to carefully outline the exits they might desire in the life they have. Each of you has a life chart. The chart may say that if the soul is not on its path at age twenty, it may experience a car accident to awaken the soul. The car accident is an exit option. You could physically die in the accident or just have a broken arm. The soul makes the decision when it is on Earth. The soul in the physical body does not know why it makes the decision. The soul may say: I've had it. I no longer want to be on this place. Or, the soul may say to the physical body—I must keep trying. I came to fulfill and override this problem. So, they stay. That is why each soul has five exit points.

Should that soul—in the accident that I speak of—choose to leave, and it is not time to leave, or if the soul could have stayed and fulfilled the life, and it comes back home then in debriefing process, this soul will be strongly and sternly, spoken to. Because the circumstances were there for the soul to continue the life and learn from it but the soul took, what we call, the easy way and left. The soul has the right to that choice. The soul may choose to leave. *But, on the Council, I, as the presiding person, always speak to the soul and say do not leave the body too early when you can work through the situation. If you come back home, when you could have gone on and corrected the situation, you will be dealt with sternly. That is done in some cases. This is not done in the case you call suicide.*

31

Suicide is when the soul is so desperate, so confused, and so lost, that it cannot function. We do not encourage suicide. However, we understand.

We are speaking of the soul of baby being prepared for birth. All souls the Council speaks with are given much information. The council speaks to souls so they will be prepared. As Celonious said to you, we turn back many. This is because this may not be the right time for the soul to enter the Earth. The parents may not be ready for this soul. This soul may not fit the situation that has changed since the parents went to Earth. That is our duty, to make sure that contracts of all still exists as written. We are not lawyers. But it is very important to read the contract of father and mother or sometimes, just mother, and see if the same contract still exists. Is the contract the same as the soul of baby wrote? Does the soul of the baby desire to enter that type of life? If not, then we cancel the contract for the soul that was to be the baby.

We, as a Council, are very selective. We must be very thorough in our work to make sure the soul going to Earth is going for the purpose that contract states. It is highly important to Celonious that this point is made. The screening process is done by at least four committees occurs before the final clearing by the Council. The Council completes the screening and makes the final decision. We read and ponder, as you would say, all recommendations. We look and read all contracts.

Now, Celonious knows that you desire to know about Dark Energy entering babies. Celonious already gave you that information. We do not assist Dark Energy. They find a human that is on drugs, a human distracted from its path or not on path, and they enter the unborn baby. This is sad, very sad.

Grace: Excuse me, the Dark Energy—does their DNA change? Does their DNA and cell memory stay like Creator gave it or does it change?

Celonious answered: Creator gave DNA to all souls made. The Creator gave all souls free will. Those of Dark Energy use free will to do wrong things. However, let Celonious make the statement to you for you to think about. Without Dark Energy's presence, many of the charts, many journeys would not be fulfilled. Dark Energy must have a negative—for a positive—to achieve spiritual growth. The positive energy must have an opportunity to stray but choose not to stray. The positive must have an opportunity to seek Creator. *The opportunity would not be present if the Dark Energy did not exist. Celonious does not approve of Dark Energy. However, it serves its purpose.*

We, on this side—as we prepare souls to enter Earth—stress to each soul that Dark Energy will exist. *We also give to each of you how to recognize Dark Energy.* As human bodies, you do not recall, but inside, the soul knows. Humans make statements like, "I had a feeling or a light went off." That is us tuning into your soul and saying to you this is the Dark Energy we speak of.

Excuse me. I have a question. I am curious about the Dark Energy human. If a physical sample of blood, skin or brain were taken would their DNA be the same as other humans?

Celonious answered: They have DNA from Creator that will be the same as other humans. You're correct. It would show as human elements show. It would be very nice if it showed bad, stay away. All would shun it and it would be exiled from the Earth.

I said that I have seen television programs that featured abnormal brain scans of criminals. Slight differences were noted, as I recall.

That is correct. Also, let Celonious say this to you: Many good souls are on Earth but some are of the weak nature of pleasing others. Some are not structured strong enough. They may be of an older age—in the thirties or forties age—and be of a weak nature in the soul. Their souls may become weak, not strong. As they sleep, and the soul leaves the body to come back home, the Dark Energy can come into the human body and take over.

When that happens—and it happens a lot—that soul must stay with us and go through debriefing, as in a death. The Dark Energy soul takes over. Then, this is when you hear frequently on Earth: What happened to this person that was very nice? They may become murderers. That is what Celonious tells you. They take over human bodies of weak souls that leave for visiting us. They keep the body. The body changes suddenly, which is true. The Dark Energy inhabited a good human body that a good human soul had been in. The Dark Energy took over and it is not the same.

Now also, while Celonious speaks of this, what you call bipolar or multiple personalities, the same thing happens. I understand and know that you in the room understand this, but others may not. As each human sleeps, the soul comes home for joy, to be back home. They have the opportunity to do.

Dark Energy does not come back to us. It stays in the human body knowing that if it leaves the human body—the Light soul—the one with us may come back. So, the Dark never leaves once it occupies the body. The human body is a house for them so they stay in it. That is when you hear that the human body of Light sleeps but the bipolar body never sleeps. That is Dark Energy that has pushed the Light Energy away. But eventually, with medication, the bipolar sleep and the Dark Energy leaves the body, then the good soul returns. This is not just bipolar but multiple personalities. It is not a disease. It is the transferring of souls into a body that has been obsessed or taken over. Do not become frightened of this because there is a way to protect yourself and loved ones. *(See Part III for how to protect yourself and loved ones).*

I, Grace, have another question and this may be too far into another field. Does this apply to organ transplants—say an organ from an evil person into a good person? Could the dark energy impact the good person in a negative way?

Celonious said, "Absolutely. It is transferring Dark Energy cells into another human body and it can become a control factor." I must go now. With your permission, I will come back next time. Also, Oshinbah is gone but asked me to tell you that he will come back next time with me and talk more to you. Celonious asks for you to write questions if you need answers. Answer will not be given unless you have questions. End

4

Oshinbah and Celonious—Questions and Answers

Today is June 25, 2010. I spoke with Naomi for a few minutes about the session of last week and the visitors we are to receive today. I presented two dreams for interpretation and then Oshinbah appeared.

Oshinbah

Oshinbah asked permission to enter and of course I said yes. Oshinbah said: I come today as I said I would do. Oshinbah has information from Creator. The changes in the Earth are close. They are fast approaching. You will hear more of earthquakes and volcanoes.

I was here before with Celonious and he is here today. First I have messages from Creator, which He asked me to repeat to you. Messages are brief. Creator wishes you to know that the book on cell memory is to be finished because of earth changes accelerating. Information for cell memory book is being given to in different ways. Some may come as dreams, Oshinbah may give a tiny bit of information, but book must be compiled, presented and finished before end of present year 2010, if possible. Oshinbah also presents to you that there will be given to you more dreams concerning events and more dreams for direction. Oshinbah is not a messenger but Creator requests that Oshinbah obey.

Now, Creator had a conference with Jamiah, Oshinbah, and your wonderful friend Elijah. This happened just before I came to you. Creator met with us about planet Earth. He spoke of that which is occurring and that which will be. Creator spoke of those who are involved in preparing others for changes. Examples are you, in your books, and others who go around the world and speak.

Creator gave Oshinbah information about the one you call Naomi. Oshinbah knows that she never recalls, so Oshinbah asks that pretty lady inform her. Creator desires and expects this to be carried out. Sessions will be shortened. Creator says the one we speak through is physically able and mentally able but those who come to her—all who receive information—must learn to shorten their sessions. In Earth time, the one we speak through will not be in this area. She will be moving around. In other words, Creator wishes to prepare those who come for information that this one will not be available. She will be on journeys. Therefore, Creator feels that to allow humans to prepare for her absence—sessions will be shortened. Requests should be kept simple and given quickly. Creator is observing that requests, not orders, are carried out. To clarify the statement: The one we are speaking through will not be available in this area. She will be on journeys.

Oshinbah asked Creator: Do I talk too long? Creator said no one talks too long. Just say what is to be said and carry on. That's the only way Oshinbah knows how to say it and to get information correct. I do not know time, as Earth has time. On this side, all who meet with Creator know when we are to stop. Creator sends a signal. When we get the signal, we stop. Creator did not say how many of Earth minutes or hours but to just shorten time. So Oshinbah must obey and stop now. Celonious has much to say.

Oshinbah, with help from this side, will be reminded to cease at a certain point. Whoever is speaking with you Jamiah, Elijah, Oshinbah, Celonious, or whoever is speaking, will be stopped. There is no time here but Creator goes by events and has specifications of what to say—for us. We are to brief you on Earth changes, on the process of birth—how souls are selected and then we are to depart.

Now, we do not have means of stopping you. It is in your own way to know to stop. Keep this in mind. This is to be done. Somehow Creator will stop this from continuing. I do not know how. I just know Creator said it would cease.

Creator is trying to train those who come here (clients of Naomi) seeking information. He is trying to train them—not just to shorten the information they need—but train them to receive.

Creator also wants this information to be passed on and given to all. This will be brought up at your next "Gathering." Throughout the world, there are groups that have begun gathering to study what you call information. Creator does not care if you do this. *Creator does care about the outcome of group meetings.*

Creator said that today there is much wrong information. In other words—if Jamiah, Oshinbah, Elijah talk with you and say to you—volcanoes, earthquakes will happen and you go to a meeting and several there have discussion—"well I don't think it will happen here, or there, or I feel like it will be this or that"—the information gets distorted.

Basic information that is given by us comes from Creator and should not be analyzed. It comes from the direct source of Creator. When analyzing of words that are spoken through (Naomi) the one we use—then incorrectly—people feel their own conscience gives direction on what they feel it means. That is okay to feel this. But, when you convince all that exist with you, that their thinking is wrong or their thinking should be altered, then you are interfering with Creator's direct issue. Therefore, Creator discourages group meeting for that purpose. Creator won't stop group. Creator said for Jamiah to inform. Creator gave free will to all souls. Creator is just giving information—so all who gather and speak of different views— so that all be aware if view be totally opposite or different or conflict with Creator's directive, then it is wrong to convince others that this is correct.

Now, outcome would be when soul crosses over. Then in the chambers—where review of events in life occurs—there would be much for soul to deal with. Each individual soul is on its own journey. Creator understands being curious about what is happening. Therefore—each soul—must determine on its own what is necessary to adopt into its thinking. Danger of group meeting is strong personalities can be persuasive over those who are less strong.

It is better for each soul to stay with its own feeling. Because, you see, each soul must learn a certain thing. Talking about it in a group does not allow this soul, or this soul to learn its lesson—it learns the view of others. Each soul, for its own heart, learns all it needs.

I said that has been my feeling and my reason for writing the books as I have. I have given, to the best of my ability, exact words of those that channeled through. I used a digital recorder and then typed the words. That way, those who read the books have the same words I received. How they interpret them or respond to them depends upon their frame of reference or experience. If the words cause a response within a person, then no discussion is needed. The information is for each soul from Creator. Each may respond differently because no two paths we walk are the same.

Oshinbah said: Group discussion is not healthy, not with this. Group discussion is not healthy with words that come from Creator or those who bring messages from Creator. Free will is a gift. Oshinbah knows that if many are gathered, not all will agree. That is where problem comes—they begin—this could not be right—and question Creator. Creator is right!

I asked if religion came about by group meetings and discussions. Oshinbah replied: Yes. Religion is not of God. God does not approve of religion because religion caused distance from God—same with what you speak of—it takes away from purpose.

Oshinbah answered: If someone asks about the books, request of the individual—think upon it—ask for clarity by dream—and your spirit guide will give an answer. It is not that you don't have correct answer, but even with correct answer, your correct answer becomes another answer to them. They then take your words and change them, and change thinking.

Oshinbah has spoken too long and is not happy with self. Celonious will now answer questions only. He gave much information last session.

Celonious

Celonious said: Celonious is here for you today and very proud that the one I speak with has desire to learn much more of that which I have in my education—on souls entering into a form.

I have been instructed that I will not be speaking long. We may have to continue if you have many questions. I feel that I presented a clear version of how souls enter into the world. You may ask questions now. I will try to answer.

I said, yes you did make it clear how souls enter a form. Does the soul choose the time to enter a fetus?

Celonious answered: They make the decision before the parents enter Earth. Those who are to be parents of soul, they all three agree. The soul does not get summoned until the conceiving.

I present this question for Naomi. It concerns the soul that has contracted to come into the fetus. Suppose the fetus is already growing in the mother, but the soul had not entered the baby. The Council reviews the contracts and discovers that the contract has to be voided. Would this create an opening for dark energy to enter the fetus?

Celonious: That would be possible except that we foresee this and have other plans in place in case something does happen. The parents, the humans before they entered earth, and the Council, which I preside over, have other plans in place.

If this did occur with anyone, we review other souls that may wish to serve the same purpose, or wish to learn the same lessons that the first soul did. We review in other words, these other souls that could or would be acceptable to enter these human lives.

If we can find and normally we do find a soul—with less spirituality—in other words, the situation that may have gone a little astray—the first soul may have been of a higher spirituality—we adjust that and allow one of a lower spirituality—as in a second or third level of vibration.

That would serve a purpose of allowing a lower vibrational level soul to advance its soul growth. For sake of comparison, let's say, it might be going into a life of more rigid standards.

Now, so far, since the beginning, since God first created—with our standards and preparations—we feel that it will stay that way—we have included in our doctrines how to select an alternate soul. We have never had a failure in doing so—failure meaning—we were able to place the soul.

How they did on their spiritual journey after they got placed and got into the human body on Earth with the parents and families is up to the individual soul. It is complicated but it is simple. It is a fast process for us. You think your computer saves you time. Ours is much faster, we think it and it is there. It is not a problem. The only problem is the advanced soul does not get to take the journey and we have to send it back to whatever journey it is doing on this side.

I said when I get confused or what confuses me is when I try to think of the physical form separate from the soul. I am not sure that I am doing this right. I am trying to get everything accurate to go into the book and at the same time, I am trying to understand it myself so I can express it properly.

Celonious said: I understand this.

I said I am trying to write something that will be helpful for the present and future people. When I think of the scientists who came to earth and made the cells, my mind goes there and I want to know all about how they did it. What is in the wall of the cells? How was it all put together? Did the cells made by scientists—just tissue—have a soul? And in my perception, they would not have because the soul had not entered the physical being. Am I on the right track?

Celonious replied: You are out of my field on the composition of the cell. But concerning the souls we send to be on certain areas of the Earth, those of the scientific field or those of higher learning from other planetary systems, had perfected a dwelling place for the soul.

That is what we refer to. Your human body, or whatever the structure or form, is a dwelling place for the soul. The soul was already prepared before scientists perfected a form. So yes, the first that was perfected, was a vessel that the soul could dwell in. The soul did dwell in it, yes.

To clarify further, I said the physical form was over here and the soul over there and the soul had to come to the physical form.

Celonious said: Correct. Let's use the simple form. On your Earth there is an egg. I speak of animals—like what you call a chicken or a snake—that lays eggs. The egg has the potential to have a soul in it—if it develops into a form. As an egg, it does not. It does not. Once it is prepared and is a dwelling place for a soul, and once it begins growing—at any time, any animal—reptile or human, begins growing—the soul primarily hovers around the area of the form that it will enter. The majority of souls of humans, animal, reptiles or whatever, do not occupy that form, they prefer not to enter the embryo system, until the last of the formation. In other words, in the case of humans, it is the last few days and in many forms, it is after the form is expelled from the body—usually, upon the first breath—they occupy. They do not like the confinement.

I said now, with the animals—I know they have DNA—do they have cell memory also? Celonious said no. Animals and reptiles exist in only one lifetime. This should be clarified. The one that I am speaking through has never been given this information. And many animal lovers come to her and their deceased animals come to visit the previous owner through her. But this has never been explained to her until now. I don't feel that you are an animal owner so this will not benefit you. It may benefit acquaintances of yours if you wish to speak of this to them.

The animals that do have one life and cross over have "spoken" through the one I am speaking through many times. When the human owners of these animals cross over, the first to greet them is an animal. What has been omitted is that they are reunited with that animal that crossed over. It stays with them on the other side. The animals do not return—theirs is a one-life thing. They do not have need for DNA or cell memory. They have a structure in their cells that indicates their differences—like a horse is different from a cow. That is their DNA. It is different from that of humans.

I am being told that I must leave. Would you like for me to return? Do you have many questions?

I said yes, I would love for you to return. I am just trying to sort out for this book what would be important information for the future. What information would be important for us to know? What for example would be the right way to handle deviants in society—like killers, murderers, and such—if we are not to control each other, how are we supposed to deal with that?

Celonious replied: The majority of those you refer to as killers and criminals, have been obsessed by Dark Energy. You can't stop them. You can't prevent that. That is part of the lessons of life. The Dark Energy will be omitted from your planet once the Earth changes occur. As you grow in the spirit, your dwelling place will not be one that has Dark Energy. They can only survive in areas that allow up to the third vibrational level. You are outgrowing them.

I understand that, I answered. But, in the meantime, during the earth changes, do we need to have guns and such to protect ourselves while they are still here. Will they try to kill us, or rob us?

Celonious: Understand that this is not my field. I am only here to speak of the souls coming to Earth. I will answer because I do know the answer. As earth begins its changes, the Dark Energy will be desperate but they will not have the capability of doing all of this because they are being taken from the Earth and many will be removed before the changes. That is why vast numbers are leaving in wars and other events.

I do not know who will be here next time. I must go now. Goodbye and good day. End

5

Edgar Cayce: Creator is Energy; DNA of Soul is Energy

Since 1980, I've read many books by or about the famous Edgar Cayce. *There is a River* by Thomas Sugrue is a good starting point to learn about him. Cayce became known as the "sleeping prophet" of our time. He discovered that he was able to help sick people to recover from their health problems. After Cayce reached adulthood, he discovered that he could lie on a couch, go into a sleep-like state, and contact the universal conscience or the superconscious. From there he could obtain information on most subjects. (In channeling, I have now learned that this state involves the soul.) He believed that in order for the physical to heal, the soul had to heal first.

Cayce learned that he could lie on his couch and view a sick patient, even if that patient was many miles away. He could diagnose the illness and prescribe correct treatment. While in his sleep state he could also see and describe the wallpaper and objects in the patient's room. Sometimes his prescribed treatment involved unusual or obsolete drugs or items. In such cases, he told patients where to find the item and how to use it. Patients that followed Cayce's directives usually healed. Although Cayce had no medical training, physicians referred many cases to him, cases that they were unable to cure and that they considered to be incurable.

A unique part of the Cayce treatments included lifestyle changes in diet, changes in attitude, and changes in behavior. Some of his teachings about diet dealt with how combinations of certain foods created acids in the system, which in turn, caused inflammation and other problems. The attitude and emotions were also very important issues. Negative thoughts, such as anger and fear, have a negative impact on the endocrine system, the circulation, and elimination. In essence, Cayce believed in balance in all things. This is an oversimplified statement as his instructions for each client were very specific and detailed for that person's problem.

Cayce's gift of visions and prophecy appeared early in his life as he grew up on a farm in Kentucky. He talked to imaginary friends and could see his deceased grandfather. He was considered different or unusual among his playmates and adults. He was raised in a religious home environment and, as an adult, became disturbed when he learned that he had spoken of reincarnation while in a trance state. In time, he came to accept reincarnation.

Cayce could never remember what he said while he was in a trance. His wife or his secretary kept records of what he said. Eventually, many of these records were transcribed and published in books. A center devoted to his work is the Association for Research and Enlightenment in Virginia Beach, Virginia. Books based on his forty years of client readings cover such topics as: reincarnation, dreams, philosophy, the pyramids, spiritual growth, the paranormal, prayer, emotions, auras, diets, weight control, and osteopathic or chiropractic adjustments for improved circulation and elimination. (http://www.edgarcayce.org/are/edgarcayce.aspx)

In the present day, Cayce frequently channels through Naomi. He was, and still is, famous for his predictions. He predicted that in the nineteen-eighties cataclysmic events would occur that would change the Earth. These did not occur and he was criticized for that error. There is an explanation, however: His predictions of events were accurate but the timing was off. The Other Side has no time but Cayce did not know that at the time of his predictions. Edgar Cayce recently channeled that Creator had summoned him to predict the Earth changes because of all the work that Cayce had done previously on that subject. His prior predictions are occurring now—the earthquakes, tsunamis, volcanic eruptions, floods and other devastating events. The Creator allowed him to come forth and inform Earth of what is happening.

Edgar Cayce

On July 30, 2010, Naomi and I discussed information channeled recently. Our discussion stopped when she sensed an energy approaching and started to channel the entity.

This is Edgar Cayce. May I enter? We do not eavesdrop on your conversations. Your spirit guide summoned me and said that it is very important that I come today. I have no clue to what she is referring except I did arrive as you were speaking of the universes and planetary systems. Those of Earth know me, as Edgar Cayce and I will speak as Edgar Cayce today.

I am positive that Athena and those of this side know of my extensive travels to other universes, much like your friend Elijah. He is now doing much traveling in a different sense that I did. This is difficult to explain. You see, Creator made each of us out of a spark or an energy cell. Each of us has our own DNA forever, and ever and ever. Even though Edgar or Elijah may go to other universes and travel throughout wherever Creator desires that we go, we still have our own basic DNA—our own cell structure that Creator gave each of us. This DNA is from Creator.

I am positive that Athena summoned me because she knew I had done extensive travel—much more so than Elijah had. Elijah is not available without Creator's approval. Elijah is not in trouble it is just that his services are demanded elsewhere. I am to shed some light or discuss what you wish to discuss. First, I am to say to you that it is highly difficult to discuss or explain in terms—as to how each planetary system or universe operate.

You are totally correct in your statements. This is recall on your part. You are correct about the information that your own cell structure has, the energy each universe has, the energy between the universes, and the container that holds the soul—whatever it may be called, is all from the Creator. Since I have not spoken with Athena—and not knowing your whole conversation—I feel it would be best for you to ask me questions so that I may enlighten you with answers you need.

Until you come up with your most important questions, I will digress and give information on what I am aware of as your concerns. The cell itself is a basic structure that holds much. We keep this basic cell. Forever and ever, throughout all eternity, we keep this basic cell structure. This is true for even the most minute of living creatures—the teeny, tiny chigger, to the largest giant—all retain the basic cell structure from Creator.

Now, scientists that are presenting on your History Channel the information they are—they are scientifically informed. However, they do not accept information about the Creator, the DNA, and where it all came from. It is informative to observe and listen to their explanations about the universes. They are correct about where they are placed and where their energies flow and all they give in that type of information. So, is there anything that Edgar could enlighten you with?

I asked, are you saying that all the DNA of humans and animals—the DNA of the physical and the soul come from Creator?

Edgar answered, the basic cell that is soul or soul cell is from Creator. The soul cell is from Creator and it expands. It expands and goes into a "container." Each universe has its own design of container—in size, in looks and so forth. On Earth, the human body is the container for each soul of the human race. Inside this container—there is the brain—the major computer, which gives instructions. Each of the other universes and planetary systems have a similar operation because Creator created all. The basic cell that Creator created from—each of us have and it directs the component—be it a brain, as in humans, or whatever it is called—to give it instructions.

That basic cell from Creator—that DNA cell from Creator is housed within a unit and gives directions. But the overriding picture is of the component that holds the soul. It makes its daily choices. Now again, it can become very complex because other universes do not expand. Now, your universe—this universe—the planet of Earth, as you know, is a school of learning for souls that wish to learn and grow at a faster pace. Not all universes have that.

There are souls who wish to just be inside a container that may just wander, that may just observe, it has its different functions in other words. To operate the container, the beginning must always be the DNA cell from Creator, no matter what container it is placed in and no matter what planet or universe or planetary system, the basic cell structure is DNA from Creator.

The human on Earth does have different cell structures—it has functions. You know this scientifically. Some of the universes do not have the expanded forms—as the human body is—it is highly complicated, as well. What I am trying to state with clarity is this: *The basic cell from Creator is what operates any and all—on any universe or on any planetary system anywhere.*

Creator is not a soul. Creator is energy. The DNA of the soul is energy also. But the DNA gives structure—so the soul can expand—and have its full meaning from Creator. The connection to Creator is necessary because Creator is always there for you to return home to. And, you are part of Creator. So, the link is there. It is like giving birth. You as a mother always have this direct contact with the child—more so than the father. It is highly complex. I am not sure that I am doing a good job.

I said: You are doing a great job. You are clarifying all those fine points that I have been seeking. Please continue!

Edgar: This is cell structure of the human body. We will not get further out than that. We will not get out into the universes and describe the creation they have, as it is of no use to you. We will eliminate that. *Just realize that the basis of all life, no matter what universe or planetary system, originates from Creator.* Beyond that we will not go because you do not need that information.

The information of the basic cell—as I was trying to explain—now let me try again. The basic cell structure from Creator is the soul—as you on Earth call the soul. The soul occupies the human body. The human body is made as a direct instruction from that first cell that split and split and split. Understand? I said yes.

From that structure, which was the basic of Creation, is the soul. The soul is housed inside the structure. Let me explain in terminology that is simple—you take ingredients to make a cake. You put them together and bake them and the end result is the baked form, which you can dress any way you choose. That is your human body. The basic ingredient—and there is only one in this case—is the cell DNA from Creator. What results—the human form that results—has within it the basic cell—just as your cake has the basic ingredients within it and when they are distributed, as a cake form, you do not see the individual ingredients.

As you form a human body from that basic cell, you do not see that basic cell but it is still there. It is what operates and keeps the human body performing. Now that is where preconscious comes in.

Once the human body is formed—and there are no mistakes by Creator—not even the splitting of the cells in the formation of the embryo—that is not a mistake. This was designed by the soul that was going to enter. The soul desired to have a form that was not perfect—an imperfect form—so it could learn its lesson. That is the difference—the lessons to be learned by souls—to be the basis—to be the pin dot that begins it all. It elected by its chart to be malformed—to learn a lesson while on earth. The cell structure of the human body is indeed of the Creator but it is from the basic cell that began it. That basic cell came from Creator. So it is like a spin-off. It is like a spider with a web—it begins here and it flows like this. It makes your human body. And that is why in your Bible it said that God created in the image of God. Not all of you on Earth look the same—so how could that be? It goes back to the basic cell. The basic cell—the DNA is in the image of God. But humans do not see this.

The terminology of religion has taken away the basic information of the soul that all humans knew in the beginning. In other words, as humans on Earth have become more and more educated, they have become less and less aware. Which is of most importance to Edgar—the awareness. The other information is secondary. It is not even necessary except to survive on the planet. Did I clarify? I said yes.

I then asked Edgar: Do animals have souls? Edgar answered that animals are of a different cell structure from Creator. You see the vision, the energy a huge energy—the energy Creator uses in animals is of a different nature. Creator chose that the animals would only have one soul—one time—one lifetime. They do have a special section for animals on the Other Side. They do go back into the system and live there forever. They don't come back onto Earth or areas of other universes. Other universes, and I will try to keep this simple—have different "pets." They have other formations, which may be rocks and that gets complex but that is where their energy may lie—as in a pet rock or a butterfly, insects. It gets really complex to go to other universes so we will stay with our own. That is what happens to animals. Animal owners who have treated the animals as part of the family will see the animals when they cross over. The animals will greet them.

You are doing a tremendous job on this book. You may quote me, not that I feel it would impress anyone, but you may quote Edgar on coming and giving you information if it will help you. It is Edgar speaking information from the Other Side that perhaps others are not aware of. I said and you are well known on Earth, even now. I have and will continue to quote you. Thank you.

I then asked Edgar the same question that I asked Celonious recently but he did not have a chance to elaborate. The question was this: If a person receives a transplant from a criminal, a killer or such, could the recipient be influenced by the bad behaviors—the cells of the organ of the criminal. Celonious had said: Absolutely! Our session had to suddenly end because of our time factor.

Edgar answered I was not present when Celonious was here. I am associated with him and he is highly informed. May I give my answer? I said of course.

The transplant of an organ or a portion of the body would depend upon that particular organ. Now, if it was a heart transplant of an organ from a dark energy—a murderer—or someone who committed a horrible act—the heart controls the emotions—then it would be likely that individual recipient might pursue this. However, if it were a kidney, it would not effect. So, far as I know, on earth, they are not transplanting brains, which is your major instructor.

Now, in screening the hearts of those of dark energy, very few of the dark energy would have a healthy heart for a transplant. Their hearts may not necessarily be damaged but there would be something wrong that would not allow it to happen.

You see Creator has a way of making sure the organ received is not contaminated this way. The characteristics of emotions are also received through other organs—kidneys, livers, etc. and also could be in the sensory—the fingers or feet but they are not of the type that would be detrimental to others. It might persuade them to want a food or an activity. The brain is the controller of most of these but they might dictate the smaller things like color preference, or taste. Again, we are speaking of cells. Each organ has its own cells and it will transfer to the individual the desire for the minute things such as clothing, foods and social life but not the emotional part that is dictated by the brain that gives instruction on action.

I do need to return now. I would like to comment. This is a highly complex universe. The book you are writing is highly important. The material is diverse and those assisting you from this side dictated the information that you have gathered. The things coming to you—such as I am giving—are screened and are very accurate. Do not have a fear of misrepresentation. They are taking care of this. I am looking forward to aiding you in some of this. Athena was great in this. She is in the Hall of Records.

6

Jamiah: DNA Connects All Souls

On 8/27/2010, Jamiah came to speak through Naomi. He again had a message from Creator about DNA and cell memory and it is typed as it was received.

Creator say to Jamiah, go visit ladies. Creator says that he will give Jamiah message by thought when he arrives. Jamiah asked Creator why He does not just tell you the message. Creator says his energy vibration is too high. He must come through lady that channels and give her thoughts and she must speak thoughts to you. If Creator gave to you directly, you would explode. It is very complicated but Creator knows best. Jamiah humble and honors Creator's choice.

Creator has information for your book. Creator says you are doing a good job. Creator says the information in your book is not just for Earth. Information in your book is about all galaxies. Creator is giving Jamiah information to give you about the cell. Put this in your book.

You are writing about cells and when Creator made souls he started with one cell. You were already told that the human cell has cell memory and DNA. And, DNA is in all of souls throughout all universes. It is important to Creator that this be written as Creator says:

"All DNA strand have connection with every soul. Each soul has strand of DNA from Creator that is alike.

Creator says He will explain how He thinks you will understand. Vegetables—He using example something he calls bean. He says kidney, green, lima beans—all are beans but all are different—but in center, all the beans are the same. Creator says use illustration because that how souls in all universes are—strand of DNA in center of cell. All, even though the outer shell of soul in other universes are a

51

different form—in center—they are the same. The center is strand of Creator." I asked if the center of the cell is called the nucleus.

Jamiah: "That name what Creator mean but he want explanation in book be very, very simple. So, that why Creator use the bean example. Creator say you know but Jamiah still not know. Other people have explained to you that strand of DNA center that you call nucleus is activated where you are on a pattern—pattern of soul—all cells. When cell memory formed after life, after life, after life—different place, different city, different planet, different universe—still cell memory. *Little tiny part you call nucleus holds all information for all eternity.*

So Creator says that nucleus—that you mentioned—is the key to all formation. But, pretty lady, Creator says it connects with all universes, all planets and any beings on all planetary systems. That important. That highly important. Creator say this must be given in books so there is understanding. When cell is not on Earth—Earth being a school—when cell occupy object—on other planet—like where Elijah go—one planet way off in area no one know—life there is contained in what looks like a ball of powder. So that cell contained in ball of powder has the same DNA cell memory—same nucleus as you—a human on Earth. Creator try to explain simple, complex, superior, all common denominator—nucleus.

Pretty lady already know Creator. Why you say again? Creator say use many examples in book so Creator have Jamiah come today and give different example—bean, beans. Okay Creator say: Nucleus in bean, nucleus in tree, nucleus in frog, nucleus in leaf, nucleus in rock, all same. They're known on Earth as inanimate objects but still have Creator in it. You know what Creator say. Jamiah have no clue what Creator mean.

Jamiah do good job? Maybe if pretty lady understand then Jamiah not have to come and repeat. But Jamiah likes coming to see pretty lady. Creator not talk directly to anyone except by thought. He talks a lot by thought but no one listen. They call it imagination. You are not like others you listen to Creator. Creator is more than what has been described. Not even Jamiah can describe Creator. Not any way to explain size or look of mass energy. Creator is mass energy—beginning, end, everything—Creator is Love. Creator unhappy that human not explain Creator is love—and use as control. Human use Creator to control, in what is called religion, and try to control others. It is not that way on other planets, just that way on school planet. But you see, on school planet, you learn wrong because of teachers not giving right information.

Creator say, Jamiah, ask pretty lady if she need help or have questions. If she needs help, you help her before you come back. So Jamiah follow Creator order. Help you?"

I said I think I understand most of what has been said. If I keep in my thoughts that Creator is energy and soul is energy and that is how we are all connected, I am okay. If I try to separate things and ask what is not of Creator, like evil or that kind of thing, then I get confused.

Jamiah said: "Creator made all souls. In beginning no evil. Soul changed after leaving Creator. Creator gave right to all souls to make choice. Some make wrong choice. Evil very bad. But evil serve purpose—allows White Light people to grow by making more vibrational spirit. Without challenge from evil, not grow as fast. Choice right you grow, choice wrong, you go to lower vibration. Vibration has much to do with spiritual growth." End

Part II

DNA and Cell Memory Connections

In this section we have more contributors, such as Isaac Newton, Galilei Galileo and Sigmund Freud and Carl Jung. (According to channeled information, while they do not channel, background assistance is provided by numerous others souls, among them Dr. David Livingstone, famous Scottish missionary and explorer and several famous authors). Dr. Freud noted the important work Dr. Nostradamas and Edgar Cayce have done with my husband over the years and this has also helped me in the cell memory work.

In prior years of channeling, it was given that my husband and I are very different in our planets of origins and our soul development. My husband is among the highest of intellect, and I am among the highest of emotional development. We charted to be together at this time, as the Earth changes occur and our development will eventually merge. As I understand it, he is learning the different emotions and I am growing intellectually. All souls on Earth are here to learn. Our experience in working with channeled material is an illustration in progress of how things work between the present Earth and the Other Side. *The message is about how things work*, not us.

My practice with clearing cell memory goes all the way back to the beginning of this channeling experience. Although in the beginning, I had no clue where it would lead. People channeled information and I had no idea what connection would follow. For example, today is January 13, 2011, and this message was *received on November 3, 2003*, when Edgar Cayce brought with him Sir Isaac Newton and at a later time, Galileo. They had messages about cell memory connections to the universe. Also, they asked that I create separate files for cell memory work.

Also, repeatedly I was told that my life experiences are what I wrote to experience so that I would understand the difficulty and the correct approach to clearing cell memories. Why did I do this? In channeling, I was told that one of my jobs on the Other Side is working with cell memory cases that are the most difficult to clear. This was one of the reasons for this incarnation.

1

Edgar Cayce: Dreams/Visions Connections

Edgar Cayce assured me that I had indeed chosen to do this cell memory work before my birth and that I will be permitted to continue this work. He said that I had chosen the field of nursing, which placed me close to the field of cell memory but it was not acknowledged at the time.

On 11/3/2003, Cayce stated, "my information for you is that there will be presented to you, in visionary form, or in the sleep state, or in the meditative state—in the presence or in the effort of visionaries—the total explanation of cell memory—how in the present state that it is in today's times—it is being used. You are very knowledgeable on this. You will find that *it will appear unto you articles out of nowhere*—much as the *graduation caps* that your dear friend Elijah has informed you of. The articles will be a confirmation—as the red-haired angels you once spoke of were a confirmation to you. Those on this side that we call "on the scientific level" will give this from this side.

We give information and cures directly to those of the medical profession on Earth. We give to those who will accept the information and use it with purity—not as greed or as a way of manifesting their abilities. *The same will be provided to you on cell memory. You may ponder upon the thought how did I know this. I knew it but how did it come here.* Much the same as the medical field—scientific research people are experimenting and surely they are—just as these experiments would come to naught if we were not here on this side putting into their brains the information they need. The same will apply to you on cell memory.

It is necessary to put these thoughts and visions in writing because the information you have in the vision, the thoughts or the articles presented to you will then be used in conjunction with people's stories as they tell them to you—the actual facts that have occurred—*of the cell memories being activated by the transference of organs to different bodies.* Now, Sir Isaac Newton wishes to speak briefly."

2

Sir Isaac Newton: Cell Memory/Universe Connections

Who was Sir Isaac Newton? He was a "mathematician and physicist. He was one of the greatest intellects of all time." . . . He attended Cambridge University and was a brilliant student. His involvement with Cambridge continued for several years after his graduation. "He held many offices as a student and later as a professor at Cambridge. He considered his years at Cambridge to be the height of his creative power. He wrote the Philosophiae Naturalis Principia Mathemataica (Mathematical Principles of Natural Philosophy commonly known as the Principia)." (http://www. newton.cam.ac.uk/newtlife.html)

"As a firm opponent of the attempt by King James II to make the universities Catholic Institutions, Newton was elected Member of Parliament for the university of Cambridge to the Convention Parliament of 1689 and set again in 1701-1702. Meanwhile, he in 1696, he moved to London as Warden of the Royal Mint. He became Master of the Mint in 1699, an office he retained until his death. He was elected Fellow of the Royal Society of London in 1671, and in 1703, he became President, being annually re-elected for the rest of his life. His major work, Opticks, appeared the next year; he was knighted in Cambridge in 1705." Ibid.

Newton did a great deal of work on how things work in the universe. He developed what we now accept at the Laws of Gravity. He developed mathematical computations for how planets orbit. He studied the theories of others and compared them to his own research. He tried to reconcile, in his own mind, the relationship between God of the Bible and His creations in the universe with his own scientific theories of how things worked. Therein lay the problem of religion versus science. Those of pure religion felt God did everything and that the Bible was somehow not in the realm of science, or said another way, it was the Big Bang theory of man versus the Bible version of Creation. Ibid.

While still a student, Newton became interested in optics. He read the works on optics of Robert Boyle and Robert Hook. He also studied the mathematics and physics of French philosopher and scientist Rene Decartes. He investigated the refraction of light by a glass prism; and over the years, developed measurable mathematical patterns of color. He found white light to be a mixture of infinitely varied colored rays (manifest in the rainbow and the spectrum) . . . . He conducted and documented numerous experiments and again, was met with harsh criticism. He developed the reflective telescope. He finally wrote the book *Optiks* (*Optics*), but he withheld its publication until after the death of the critics. The book was not perfect; "the colors of diffraction defeated Newton. Nevertheless, Opticks established itself, from 1775, as a model of the interweaving of theory with quantitative experimentation." Ibid.

By his own account, Newton taught himself about mathematics by studying the works of others. He made contributions to all branches of mathematics. He is probably best known for his theory of gravity. According to a now famous story, Newton was in his orchard and saw an apple fall, and from this, he conceived that the same force governed the motion of the moon and the apple. He calculated the force needed to hold the Moon in its orbit, as compared with the force pulling an object to the ground. Ibid.

Regarding religion, "Newton wrote on Judaeo-Christian prophecy, whose decipherment was essential, he thought, to the understanding of God. His message in his book on the subject was that Christianity went astray in the fourth century A.D., when the first Council of Nicaea propounded erroneous doctrines of the nature of Christ. His beliefs were unorthodox. Although a critic of accepted Trinitarian dogmas and the Council of Nicaea, he possessed a deep religious sense. He honored the Bible and accepted its account of creation and in later years spoke of God's providential role in nature." Ibid. End

Sir Isaac Newton Channeled:

On 11/3/2003, Isaac Newton stated: I do wish to be brief. I do not have the experience or vibrational level that Edgar has. The information I wish to impart to you is the scientific means of acquiring the cell memory. I am speaking to the one that Edgar called Grace. *The scientific means has already been given to the medical community. They have withheld them, as if there was a foolish interpretation of them.*

I also wish to impart to you that the purpose for which *God ordained me was to give you information. I am to tell you how the dimensions, the universes, the galaxies, and the planetary systems are all intertwined.* I am being brief. The reason I am doing this is that the intertwining of the galaxies, the universes and the planets have a very similar connection.

All of the cell memory that you are undertaking to study—information gained—is intertwined with the galaxies, universes and planets. *This is a universal, galaxy, planetary system—the cell memory is ordained throughout all of God's work—all that God has done and completed. Cell memories are also in inanimate objects such as trees, rocks, flowers, and earth—there are cells that compose these. We will not discuss this* at this time and probably never. It has no bearing on what your work will be. So, we will proceed with what I came to say, which is to let you know that the cell memory—in the scientific world—will not be acknowledged as much or as thoroughly—as that, which you present to your planet.

The works you are to present are one of utmost importance throughout galaxies and universes. Do not be frightened by this. We know the soul of you has the knowledge within already. The information will be used as a molecular structural informative nature in all galaxies and universes.

This will be presented and used to explain that God—in all of his wisdom and power—in composing the cells in an inanimate object or breathing individual—began all of the structures with the cell. The cell retains this memory; even the planetary systems retain this memory. The complications of all the explanations, if I continue on this route, will be too overwhelming.

As I stated, my conversation with you is very brief. It is to inform you that the soul of you has the knowledge, wisdom and understanding within it. As Edgar stated, once information is presented to you, it will activate all that is knowledgeable in your soul and the information will come through.

I am here to let you know that the galaxies, universes and the planets within these are magnificent beyond description. And all of it begins with the cell. God knew that it would be the beginning of each and every object that he manifested to manufacture.

Do not be frightened of this. You do not have to have multiple degrees of any nature to acquire the knowledge that you have. Acceptance will be had—reluctantly on your planet—but in the universes and galaxies, there are souls anticipating the completion of this work. Goodbye.

3

Galileo: Cell Memory, Math, Astronomy and Soul

Dava Sobel's article, "His Place in Science" describes Galileo as a loyal Catholic throughout his life. He conducted bold investigations convinced that Nature followed a Divine order. Just as the Bible represented the dictated word of God, so the natural world embodied God's work. The persistent observer could decipher its hidden patterns, on Earth and in the heavens." (http://www. pbs.org/wgbh/nova/galileo/science.html)

Galileo felt that his most important contributions were in his applications of mathematics to the study of motion. He felt this was more important than his astronomical discoveries or his published defense of Copernicus. Galileo sought "quantifiable entities such as time, distance, and acceleration to describe the way objects move, bend break, and fall. His emphasis on the practical application and value of science set him apart from most philosophers of his time."(Ibid)

Galileo said, "Philosophy is written in the grand book of the universe. But the book cannot be understood unless one learns to comprehend the language and to read the alphabet in which it is composed. It is written in the language of mathematics, and its characters are triangles, circles, and other geometric figures, without which, it is humanly impossible to understand a single word." Ibid.

Galileo discovered, described and proved by mathematical law how things occur. Other philosophers had not done this. He showed how objects of different weights fall at the same speed. He showed how the shape of a path traced through space by a hurled object or fired missile was "not just a line somehow curved," as his predecessors had said, but the shape was "always a precise parabola." He studied and developed formulas regarding the incline plane. Also, he discovered the refracting telescope. (He could see for himself that Copernicus was correct that Earth and other planets orbit around the sun.) What is amazing is that Galileo did all of these things and uncovered the fundamental relationship between distance and time without so much as reliable unit of measure or an accurate clock. Italy possessed no national standards in the seventeenth century. So, Galileo devised his own methods to calculated the things he needed to measure distance or time. Ibid.

Galileo Channeled

In Channeling, Galileo spoke with my husband and connected more information with cell memory. I have condensed what he said in this session:

> Galileo said that my present husband was once "his apprentice and had worked in different lifetimes with scientists and astronomers."

> Also, he noted that the "brilliant knowledge that he has in mathematics goes hand-in-hand with science and astronomy and this is known by this individual regardless of the state he is in—sleep, out of body or awake. All of this combines as one to determine the dimensions, the travel, the vicinity of all planets and universes. It is of utmost importance to know this, even after you leave the Earth plane." Galileo went on to express that "this lifetime, my husband is on a different mission—in short, he has chosen to work toward soul growth spiritually. A portion of this involves passing on what he knows to the different bodies selected in the Council.

> There are many different kinds of councils. To be able to impart the knowledge, the soul must be in a method of reclaiming its former identities. To gain this knowledge, when on this side, go to the Hall of Records. There is a chair that is sat on—sitting there in a chair under a brilliant light beam—all of the former lives are absorbed into the soul—so that they may renew and come forth with all the knowledge that is needed at that time. This brings cell memory back to the soul. This is complicated and hard to describe.

The Hall of Justice is often mentioned, but there is also a Hall of Knowledge on this side, which is not mentioned as often. Galileo went on to say that, in each of these areas, information located in that area—is accessed—in the chair under the brilliant beam of "light, which brings the cell memory back to the soul."

4

Dr. Freud: Introduction to Dream Work

and Cell Memory

First, an overview of the famous Dr. Freud's life: Dr. Sigmund Freud was of Jewish ancestry and born in Austria in 1939. He was first a physician trained in neurology and then he became a psychiatrist. *He is known as the father of psychoanalysis. "He is best known for his tendency to trace nearly all psychological problems back to sexual issues.* He is also known for interpreting the recorded dreams of patients. He believed that the unconscious could be brought to the conscious level. Only parts of his theory of psychosexual development are now accepted by mainstream psychology." Freud's theory of the Oedipal Complex is still recognized by most psychiatrists and other professionals. (http://www.nndb.com/people/736/000029649/)

Other innovations by Dr. Freud include but are not limited to: "the therapy couch, the use of talk therapy to solve problems, and his theories about the unconscious—including the role of repression, denial, sublimation, and projection. Dr. Freud also did extensive work with hypnotherapy. He believed that this catharsis or "talking cure" was a way to alleviate neurosis and hysteria. This led to his method of the "couch therapy" and "free association talks." Ibid.

Dr. Freud categorized and defined stages of mind development into the id, ego and superego. The *id* represents a young child's way of relating to the world. As the child grows, he becomes aware that he is separate from others people and other objects that satisfy his desires. "This self-aware aspect of the psyche is the *ego*. The psyche then gives rise to that aspect that Freud called the *superego*. The superego is the internalized sense of right and wrong, the conscience. And in contrast to the id, which is very inward focused (with its cues coming from the needs of the self), the superego is very outward focused, with its priorities driven in large part by the needs of others: one's parents, teachers, the community. Ibid.

Freud also labeled and defined how id, ego, and superego may work together in life to form *"defense mechanisms."* Among the defense mechanisms named were denial, repression, sublimation, intellectualism, compensation, and reaction formation. Freud discovered that repressed knowledge can still influence behavior. An example given was: an individual may have a body based yearning for sexual gratification, but have an internalized moral belief that says sex is dirty and sinful. The conflict between innate desire (id) and conditioned beliefs (superego) may manifest in such symptoms as anxiety, guilt, and frustration. Meanwhile, in the struggle to keep the inner peace—and balance the dictates of the superego with the demands of the id—the ego may resort to one of a variety of defense mechanisms. The conflicted individual may try to force himself to believe the moral superiority of "waiting for marriage" and become more frustrated and need to speak of this to others. Ibid.

Freud's exploration of such phenomenon, and his assertion about the nature and functioning of the unconscious mind remains one of his major contributions to the field of psychology. Prior to his work, people believed in a kind of "positivism." That means that individuals, and by extension, whole societies could live moral lives by choosing to do so. For example: to live moral lives as defined wholly by the Bible (or to live wholly rational lives as defined by science)." . . . In reality of course people have a variety of problems. "Freud offered a method through which the individual could uncover the root source of the dysfunction and, ideally, *heal it,* thus becoming freer to make better, more satisfying choices." Ibid.

Today, Freud is still recognized for his contributions on the unconscious and talk therapy. However, many major changes have occurred in the understanding of child development, gender issues, and the other drives beyond sex that shape human behavior. Also, other methods have been developed to treat dysfunction. Some schools still incorporated many of Freud's ideas. Ibid.

Dr. Freud moved from Austria to England at some point. He spent his last several years battling cancer of the throat and jaw. He had smoked cigars for many years. Ultimately he asked his physician to end his life. He died of a physician-assisted overdose of morphine on September 23, 1939 and was cremated. He was an Atheist. Ibid.

This concludes a brief account of the life of Dr. Freud. Now, the following is information that he channeled. In order to receive information about DNA and cell memory, I first had to clear out garbage from my own soul. This I discovered was being done over the years as I worked with channeled material, dreams and dream interpretations. Elijah has been my primary teacher/counselor and Athena my wonderful Spirit Guide from the beginning of this journey. Then suddenly another teacher appeared when I was having a tough time. It was Dr. Freud.

Dr. Sigmund Freud first came to channel and assist me toward the end of October 2007. He stated: In many lifetimes you have been in the position that I am in. You were in the medical field of the mind, the soul, of helping others—not only on Earth but also, on the Other Side.

You are always in the picture of helping the soul to heal—to deal with the issues that it could never deal with when it was on Earth—and not in the debriefing room, the Chambers. There is another area, in another one of the levels you go to where you are considered the best in that field.

Now, contradictory to that, is this fact—when you are on Earth—especially this time—you can't do crap about your own life. (I laughed out loud). It dangles here and dangles there. But, that is so that you may experience the emotions of humans on Earth. You will know when you go back—that you are of a more understanding nature—in dealing with those souls that have issues—and have to go back to the debriefing room—because they could not adjust and accept the concept that was being given by me and other experts, including yourself.

So, part of your lesson this time on Earth, in addition to what has been told to you, is to experience the other side of humans, the side that you work with on the Other Side. Meaning—on this side—the Other Side—you work with the souls that have crossed over that have not let go of the emotions that they felt as souls on Earth. Now, you are wading through it yourself.

This is definitely connected to cell memory work. He went on to say: *It was your choice before you came onto Earth but there is an overall purpose for the universe and the universes to learn of this. This is the main part, as it unfolds. This is the* connection and *this is what the final conclusion will be.* But, you are still working through it and that will all connect. That is, as I stated, you are on the Other Side working with souls who had these conflicts similar to what yours are. All conflicts—within humans when they are on Earth—are the fact they either feel they themselves have failed or that someone else has mistreated them. It is all a soul growth pattern.

To allow the soul growth to occur, then you have to work through the emotional state, while on Earth, of acceptance of the fact that all souls made by God are equal; and all souls made by God make errors; and all souls made by God will do stupid, silly, harmful things, when they are on planet Earth. This does not apply to other planets.

The planet Earth is your school ground. It is every soul's school ground when you enter it. So, the connection is this—on the Other Side—you are helping these souls who could not understand and work through when they were on Earth.

You have come on Earth this time to actually *experience* how it feels to have a mother that did not know how to love, and did not feel love herself, and to marry into a situation where it was even worse. You have involved and deliberately placed yourself in the center. As silly as it may sound or appear, because of the pain and hurt you feel as a human, you deliberately chose to experience this because you will gain knowledge about cell memory.

You have already been informed and seek out knowledge about the cell memory. As you *experience* what you are experiencing and *the knowledge* becomes more pertinent to your life and to lives of others, then the cell memory that the soul brings back each time, will show you the influence—of you either accepting the criticism, the hurt and the pain, or not—the denial of the hurt and the pain. *The cell memory brought back each time will show the people who can deal with and people who don't deal with these issues. This is all related to cell memory.*

Dr. Freud used Naomi as an example of one who had dealt with cell memory properly. In doing so, she advanced to another level spiritually. He described a life in which Naomi died alone in a desert. A parade of companions abandoned her. She chose not to cling to hate, frustration and anger. As she died, she chose to forgive those who could not or did not help her. Her choices at that time allowed her to elevate to where she is at present. She learned to let go of experiences that are painful and hurtful. This is cell memory. As Naomi came back to other lives, she experienced other cell memories—frustrations, problems and events. But because of the situation in the desert, and then allowing it to surface with whatever the situation she faced, she would say: Okay, I'll let that go because I have to grow myself.

This is where you are today. This is the reason for the example. When you came on Earth this time, on the Other Side, you were already highly praised. You were of the higher nature of helping those who do not understand how to deal with this and you use their cell memories. You cleanse their cell memories on the Other Side. But, you felt—to help your work on the Other Side, to improve even more—that you needed to be placed in the situation where every "hell bent" thing that existed in life, you would experience. You have.

And now, the time has arrived. You are writing a book. The time has arrived for you to recognize how to deal with this and I am helping you with it. I will continue helping you with it at night, as you sleep.

You will arrive at it. There is no other way for you to leave the Earth and come over here and help, as you wish, and as your desires are. So, you will deal with this. Now, I am not going to specify a certain time, certain place or certain event. I will tell you that your desire—this inner longing that you have had for years to explore cell memory—is because of your wanting to come down here and experience what you are now so that you might work through yourself, events that happen, and leave the earth with a cell memory that says: "Acceptance of all that is."

You don't have to approve of them. But you do have to work through to an acceptance of events that happen. When acceptance happens—then when you leave the earth—then the cell memory no longer comes back into any plane. If the soul is in any other planet or universe, when the soul takes birth, it does not experience any cell memory carry over—no matter who does what to it. It is a slate wiped cleaned. Because you learned that in this lifetime, from henceforth, there will be none of that present. But you, my dear lovely lady, chose to experience all that has and is happening with you.

Now, one of the joyful experiences happening with you—at this time—that is influencing your cell memory—is your husband's change in his outlook. Your cell memory has been with him in other lifetimes, when he has experienced events, and he has brought them forth this time. His attitude has changed with Nostradamas working with him. Nostradamas continues to help him through issues and situations involving cell memory, which he brought forth clings to but this will be erased before he departs. Yours will be erased also.

Your present experience is you observing a promotion—that of your husband. You are seeing how—when you do release cell memory and allow it to leave, you do not focus on it anymore. The cell memory in the human that is absorbed by the soul—is carried to the Other Side.

Now, this is very technical and perhaps almost not understandable. But, as time goes by, you see evidence of all. There will be documented cases that you will be studying that give you evidence of how individuals have changed.

The transplant of organs is one of the better examples we can give you, and the cell memory, in that particular organ, surfaces in the human body. Well my dear, this gives you evidence that the human body is only a vehicle for the soul to reside in.

With you, I work with you myself, along with other scientific researchers. We welcome and look forward to having you back into our fold with your new experience and new advice that you can give. But, that time is not yet to be. Meanwhile, we are thankful to have the one who channels to assist in helping you work through and continue to perfect the program that you came to do. *I will be with you almost every night.* I asked: How can I recognize you as the one working with me?

Dr. Freud answered: You will have thoughts come and you will say wow, why didn't I think of this before. I will be implanting methods of your learning of cell memory work. It is primarily cell memory work but as cell memory perfects, then physically, your human body will also will learn the lesson it needs, so that your soul will know when it goes back. All of it ties in together. I must leave. Think upon and re-examine what we have covered and prepare questions for the next session. Your recordings let you listen and re-examine. I would like you to listen over and over. We need to discuss these things.

Elijah has been called away by those who came for him. He asked that I bid you a fond farewell and he will be with you. I don't know what this means dear, but he said tell you when the hairs on your neck prickle, you will know it is him.

Also, Elijah wants you to have this information to place in your book. *When souls channel words through Naomi, it gives her soul an energized charge of knowledge, which she keeps stored somewhere in her soul, not in the surface of the human.* He believes this is new information for you. Naomi does not consciously recall this information.

5

Dreams of Author Given and Interpreted by Freud

Today is 11/16/2007. Naomi and I discussed the dreams that I've had. As requested by Dr. Freud, while I am working with him, I am to submit all my dreams to Naomi for interpretation. Through Naomi he will interpret the dreams.

On 11/10/2007, I felt like I was summoned to a bar/restaurant. The first person I saw was a young man of about thirty who was about six feet tall and wore a sky blue fitted shirt of nylon or satin fabric. It had short sleeves. He looked Asian. I placed my hands on his torso and asked: Do you know my husband? He said: Yes.

In the background, I saw the late mother of a man I used to date. She and I always loved each other. I was happy to see her looking young and happy.

Interpretation11/16/2007: This was a Polynesian life you had together. You recognized him. It was your present husband in another life. By touching his torso, as you did, and asking do you know my husband, you were asking him in the spirit form to know himself. By touching his essence, you were saying combine that essence with the current human that I know. You were asking the attributes he had in that lifetime to manifest in this one. You wanted his spirit of that lifetime to infuse into this spirit and see things in a different light. You were in the spirit world.

The woman in the background that was so fond of you and you of her, she was just an added attraction to the backdrop. She heard of your coming to the Other Side and wanted to see you in spirit form.

On 11/11/2007, I dreamed that I was in a very sunny open area, perhaps a field or park. My uncle Ben was there. He was squatting and had a child about nine months old on his knee. He and the child were laughing. He said to me, go to Bon Aqua. I think you can find the way there. Then I had an image in the back of my mind about red shoes. I am not sure if this was part of the dream. The dream felt like a combination of history and now. I awoke and recalled that someone once spoke to me of the Bon Aqua Springs being the site of an old hotel. I do not know if it is being renovated. Many years ago, this was a resort for mineral baths. I don't recall ever seeing this place.

Interpretation 11/16/2007: You both were on the Other Side. The child is deceased. You said your uncle is alive, so you both were in out of body travel. You need to seek the healing waters of life, not the Christ but things that are of a healing nature. You and my husband are both doing a lot of traveling together in dreams. Water is a symbol. Ben said you know where the springs are. In saying that, he was letting you know that you know the location of the spiritual that you need to seek more of. He is a highly evolved soul. What he was saying is seek out that which lies within you.

He is saying the knowledge of the minerals and the different things you need to know are within yourself so seek them and use them. He is a highly developed soul.

I commented that he is a lot of fun and every time I dream of him we are laughing, playing and dancing. He was very good to me when I was little. He taught me to dance. I had two younger sisters. He taught us to swim. He picked each of us up and tossed us into a concrete pool of water, which was about five feet deep. It was built beside our barn on the farm. Rainwater flowed from the barn roof into the pool. This pool insured the animals had water during times of droughts.

Ben is a more highly evolved soul than a lot of us. He is playful and knows how to have fun every day he lives and when he goes to the Other Side. He is preparing to go to the Other Side. He goes there to learn what to expect. Do not be surprised if he should cross over.

On 11/12/2007, I dreamed that my husband and I were in an open space outside where there were many rectangular tables. We passed the first tables and went to the back row. Someone placed a table in front of us. A neighbor looked at us, turned her back and said the word "good." I realized this event was for her benefit. Naomi didn't interpret this dream. However, a few weeks later, we had a tree cut between our properties and we covered all expenses.

In the middle of the night on *11/13/2007*, I dreamed of a piece of pie being placed into a refrigerator. Apparently unrelated to the first item, I saw a young black male wearing black velour pants, which he planned to wear to a party. He asked if I approved. I said yes and he seemed happy. Naomi just waved this dream aside as not important.

Two nights later, I dreamed of astral travel. I was with someone. I was "dropped off" after being on a trip. I saw a bright light with something attached leaving. The background was deep green like water instead of blue like the sky. I called out, "come back. I want to go with you." I woke up.

Interpretation 11/16/2007: Without hesitation, Naomi said Planetary System Travel (PST) is where you had been. You got to visit your homes of different lifetimes on different planets. Athena, your Spirit Guide, was with you. The Spirit Guides are with you to help you and guide you around the voids. There are voids that you can drop into. You requested to go to the different planetary systems and you have to make the request and they evaluate if you are ready for it. So you requested, and got approval and then did not want to come back here. You'll have more of this.

The last dream I had was of the basement being painted white. I was dancing with someone.

Interpretation 11/16/2007: Immediately, Naomi said, it was your son Kirk. I was shown his face. The dancing was celebrating Kirk's enlightenment and the resulting peace.

Today, just before I woke, I was jogging in a building and I was tall and healthy.

Interpretation 11/16/2007: You were out of body and in a higher elevated state. You are playing in the spirit level like your uncle Ben does. You've done a lot of soul travel this week. I said well, Dr. Freud had said that he would give me dreams and will be working with me. Naomi said: Dr. Freud is now here.

Dr. Freud

Dr. Freud: I am very surprised and pleased of your memory of the dreams and their discussion. I was surprised at the accuracy of the interpretation by the one who channels. I am pleased that she picked up on the fact that one was a fragmented and of no importance and you tossed it out. Discussion of the material of the others was very accurate. I appreciate the efforts of each party—the one that is dreaming and the one using her abilities to interpret and clarify.

Now, this past week was a drill, a practice session that is to be included in the book, number three, as you call it. This was a very successful dry run of what we will be doing. It will progress very rapidly. By the way, the PST was a very enlightening experience. I was also in the group that went with you. That is another lesson on cell memory that we will get into later.

This is going to be a book that requires a lot of thorough reading. A dedication from the public that has a desire to learn about cell memory has to be there to want this book.

I said "test" is another word that I remember from the dream. During this week, I have often said to my husband, I feel like we are part of a huge experiment or test. The dream of the flying thing, it felt like a test—something we have to do every few years. He agreed.

Dr. Freud said: Record all that you recall even, what you just said. There will be more coming during this coming week and you are to keep detailed records of the dreams. This is just beginning. This is baby-steps in approaching the cell memory. You will not be here next week. From here on, this is to be very scientific, scientific in earth terms, realistic in terms of the soul. On the Other Side it is very simple.

Meanwhile, cell memory cases that have been talked about in your presence or you have heard about, you have already documented those and you will begin to log them, case one, case two, case three, if you have not already done this. That is all for today. Do you have questions?

I, Grace, said: Yes, one paragraph from last week is not clear. You gave it right after you mentioned transplants. It was not clear so I left it out. It was about organ transplants between humans. The topic was about cell memories of the donor manifesting in the recipient of the organ. The first part of the paragraph contradicted the second part.

The second part of the paragraph seemed accurate. It stated that the donated organ does not change the soul within the recipient. I understand this to mean that the organ is only to help the physical body function. It does not change the soul or the soul memory.

Dr. Freud answered: Does not. That is correct. The misinterpretation was the one who channels gave my words twice. The sentence should have been: The organ transplanted into the human body—the physical body—triggers cell memories—it incorporates cell memories into the soul that is occupying the human body.

In other words, your physical body receives an organ donated from another human. This human might have had a habit of drinking, smoking or whatever and you may not have had that habit at that time. The physical form acknowledges and accepts those cell memories from the other body. *If you should die, with this transplant, the cell memory of the physical form itself, when the cell memory is born again into a human body it will have acquired a taste for that cell memory.*

I still had a problem with understanding this, so I said let me try this. Suppose I liked French fries and I gave Naomi an organ—she did not like French fries before—now that she has the organ—now she likes French fries.

Dr. Freud said: Correct.

I continued with this train of thought. That is because her soul self allowed her physical self to incorporate the cell memory into her physical body.

Dr. Freud said: Correct.

I said the issue that I am having with this is: Where does my soul and her soul separate? I take with me that I like French fries. She now takes with her that she likes French fries.

Dr. Freud explained that the soul is not involved. It is the cell memory of the physical. The physical manifests when the soul reenters a vehicle whether it be a human body or one from another planetary system. I replied, you're saying the physical "re-manifests." Dr. Freud said: Right. I then said: So the soul is dragging along the cell memory with it.

Dr. Freud elaborated on this comment: Well, it has the memory that manifests in the physical or it would not activate. That too can be dissipated by hypnosis or in the dream state—have another individual say—you will no longer have that memory. That removes the consciousness of "wanting the habit" or whatever the problem that exists, until you no longer have it. So, in rectifying the problem, we go back to the soul that originated, the original soul and now we are working with "solutions." In the book there will be a chapter on solutions.

Again I tried to restate my lack of understanding. My problem in understanding this was, if my soul did not have this before the organ, how much of this other person, the donor, is being transferred by the "organ." Dr. Freud said: None of the other person is transferred—just the habits—the physical part. I said: So, that other soul never touches mine. My soul does drag with it that physical cell memory though? Dr. Freud said: Yes, and it only activates when you enter another vehicle. You don't cross over and desire French fries. Not all the time. Some do.

In your state, there was a case of two twelve-year-olds. One was killed and the other one received the heart. You might discretely find out if that child has cell memories of the other one.

I apologize for the confusion. More clarification will be given. For the next ten days, we will go on many journeys. You seem to delight in these journeys. This, that you are undertaking, will be a very high challenge and I ask that you relax and meditate and we will have high assistance from this side.

I said that I feel I already know this but there is like a thin fabric or mesh separating it from me. Dr. Freud replied: the mesh you know on this side as "ectoplasm." On this side you work with that. It is an intriguing field. Very few on earth are informed because the transplant system has not existed that long on this planet. You will find that, as we journey to other planetary systems, that this system has been used for several centuries. You are refreshing your memory that is why it feels familiar.

I said, once Oshinbah said that the aliens have no emotions like we do and they are curious if our emotions cause physical ailments. I felt the other day that you were about to comment on my physical ailments.

Dr. Freud said: The aliens do not experience physical discomforts, ailments, surgeries—these aspects—because they do not have the same composition that you have. On the other hand, the emotional state has a high influence on the physical. We will discuss this later if you bring it up. I must go give lectures on this side to those who are uninformed about the mental field. I wish you a happy holiday. End

Dreams

On 11/17/2007, I dreamed of being in a gathering of about thirty people. A woman wearing a beige dress and heels appeared. She said to me by thought something about a talent show and what she was going to do. It seemed to be a game. I thought I have no talent and she probably has not talent either.

The woman stood on a hassock in the center of the room and proceeded to get the audience involved by having everyone say: "Who rocked the boat? Who rocked the boat?" She then fell from the hassock. Everyone laughed.

Interpretation 12/14/2007: I am told that you were presented a person you were unfamiliar with, which represents unfamiliar things in your life. The words she said represent how you must react when things knock you off your soul growth. The earth things, deal with it with humor. Who rocked the boat is the theme to recall when things go wrong.

On 11/18/2007, again I dreamed of being with about thirty people. Everyone was happy and friendly.

Later, I dreamed about standing next to a man that felt like a man I know. His name is Ray, a prior neighbor. He was standing in front of a waist high cabinet. There was a small notch in the cabinet about a one-inch square. By thought, he said something about sealer. I did not know if he meant sealer for his driveway or sealer for his wood cabinets—the cabinets looked sealed to me. I was awake several times during the night and know there were numerous other dreams but none stood out long enough for me to record them.

Interpretation 12/14/2007: The person in the dream is on the Other Side. He is not who you thought. I am being told the word was seller, not sealer. This has something to do with a mystic type thing. There is an opportunity to make money or advance financially. The word is seller. This was a "play on words—like sell before it goes to the cellar." It will come through when your husband comes. You are to sell something but not everything. You were approached so that you would bring the subject here.

On 11/19/2007, I dreamed something about an elderly care facility but I do not know where it was. It might have been the Other Side—everything was white—the interior of buildings, clothing people wore and the skin and hair of people.

Whether I was inside or outside everything was white. In both areas, people were taking care of other people. I considered whether I was assigned to take care of anyone. I decided that thankfully, I was not. I recalled thinking of how it takes special people to provide ongoing care for people who cannot care for themselves. Caregivers must have patience, compassion, and a healthy body to endure this. Also, the caregiver must receive positive loving energy to replace the positive energy the caregiver is giving out. Otherwise, one becomes depleted and burned out.

Interpretation 12/14/2007: You were on the Other Side but not in a health care facility. You were viewing the sterility of the debriefing area. Those you saw were those who had a lot to debrief. You saw those who were arriving and you accurately described the attributes required of those who provide the care in debriefing.

Next I dreamed something that I cannot recall and also, something about preserving papers. Then I dreamed something about a male person and also, something about his shoes, the soles of his shoes were "serrated" or a word that sounded like that. I think it had to do with trust but I am not sure. Then, I was thinking about my shrubs and the black mulch, and how the shrubs are dead, and I think the drought and black mulch combined killed the shrubs. I don't like the black mulch. I wanted the pine bark mulch. I don't know if these two thoughts were related.

Interpretation 12/14/2007: Naomi said that was a fragmented dream. The sole of shoe is a symbol of the soul—fragmented souls—and you were not permitted to recall all of the dreams. This was on the Other Side and those souls that have a lot to clear. This was a spin off of the previous areas. The souls feel torn apart and that was the meaning of the serrated shoes. This does take a lot of time to repair. You were disturbed by these souls. They will heal. These dreams are to go into a book on cell memory.

On 11/20/2007, I woke up and recorded the following dream. I was in an apartment building corridor or hospital corridor. I was positioned facing two women—I felt like I was looking down from above. The two women were discussing what looked like a set of wedding rings that each wore. The seemed to be comparing rings. They spoke of paying for the rings. They bought the rings themselves was my impression. Each woman wore her ring on the left hand. The woman to my right, as I faced her, wore a band that had very small stones. I paid more attention to that ring. Also, the circumference of this ring was smaller.

Interpretation by Naomi 12/14/2007: Someone is telling me the rings are symbolic of unity, unity of a portion of the soul back with the Creator. Some looked more valuable or had more stones. That unity was one who had more unity with the Creator. That symbolizes that the individual has achieved more, done more. They earned what they had by doing deeds or the work they came to do, which enables us to get back to our Creator.

Next, I dreamed something about a bowl sitting inside another bowl placed in a refrigerator. The first bow was round and about eight inches across and a slightly smaller bowl sat within it. The small bowl was empty. The bowls were in a refrigerator and a light went on when the door was opened. It made no sense to place empty bowls in the refrigerator. I think I placed the bowls and I think the two women with the rings were with me.

Interpretation by Naomi 12/14/2007: This was the same area as the women, just as you thought. The bowls represent what is in the Bible, the vessels of life. The bowl one within the other, represent us, we are each within the other, there is unity and your dream is all pieced together in unity. The wedding rings and the vessels all pertain to unity with the Creator. As the vessels sit within each other, so are we, as souls within each other. We benefit each other. We fit together. You placed the bowls on ice because you wanted the vessels united with each other and nothing else in them. This is a deep soul dream.

On the same day, I dreamed the following dream twice. I lived in a two-story brick house on top of a hill. The area had rolling hills. A few yards down the hill was a smaller house that faced my house. The daughter of my friend Polly lived there. The first time I had the dream, Polly and someone were on the daughter's porch asking which house was mine. They wanted to visit. I awoke and returned to sleep. The second time I dreamed this Polly again was on the porch and this time directing someone else to my house.

Interpretation by Naomi: You were elevated. Polly was proud to show others how you have grown. This was also shown on the Other Side. You are doing a lot of astral travel. This was like the souls were connected in astral travel.

The last dream was of letters of the alphabet in capital block style. There were two words—HALT HALT. The second word had letters scattered above and below the line of the first word. These words seemed to be a label on something. Naomi laughed and said, halt. That was enough dreaming for the night. They have a sense of humor. End

My activities for the day of 11/20/2007 included a doctor's appointment because of pain in my back and ankle. And to end the day, I had promised to attend the annual Thanksgiving Dinner at the local multi-level Skilled Nursing and Rehabilitation Facility or nursing home. It is a nice place. Dot, my mother-in-law, was an Assisted Living resident. She was president of a committee there, an avid reader, and had degrees in education and nursing. She lived with us four years prior to this admission.

Dot was actually better than most patients I've seen gradually deteriorate with age. Most of the frustrations are with self and a body that no longer functions well. She was determined to care for herself, had worked all her life and could afford Assisted Living. So, we had to go to dinner. We met Dot in the dining hall. She chose to sit with her back to a corner to "see the action" and be near an exit to restrooms and also be the first one out when the festivities ended. She informed us that she and the administrator were "close, like brother and sister"—she was age ninety-two and he was about forty. She proceeded to give us wrong information such as: "The pharmacy students write medication orders and have me taking experimental drugs, so, now my teeth are crumbling." We also learned that the profuse growth of her houseplant was because she fed it her potassium capsules. The facility food was excellent, as usual, and the night was pleasant because the staff worked so hard.

Finally, the night ended, as usual, with a backhanded compliment from Dot: "I see your hair is longer it looks good!" I tried to change the subject but she repeated her statement. I said thank you. Right on cue, she said: "I know you don't like having your picture taken, but lately, some of your pictures actually look good." I did not reply. We were leaving and continued out the door on our way home.

Dream

This is what I dreamed 11/20/2007, after this nursing home event. People were present but they vanished. I was standing in my kitchen alone. I thought I got a glimpse of a mouse. I looked and no mouse. Suddenly, I saw a small mouse near the dining room door. The animal went under my table. Just as I thought of how to remove the mouse, a larger one appeared. It took the smaller mouse and left.

Interpretation 12/21/2007: Whatever you think of as a mouse or rat—like something mean or nasty—most people don't want them around. Whatever you dream of an animal is what your thoughts are of that particular animal. That dream was telling you that you pictured someone or some disturbance in your life as a mouse. A rat or mouse is always someone of a negative or evil nature. They stand around and may envelope one another. There will still be negativity around. The larger one removed the smaller one, so the negativity left your house.

Next, I dreamed that I was in a building and then I went outside. I saw a small table or scaffolding of some kind. A female came. I said: I usually come out here and someone has matches. The female said: You showed your butt. You better be glad I came.

Interpretation 12/21/2007: Athena, your Spirit Guide, told you that she was protecting you and intervened to protect you. She finally reached you in the dream state.

I said to Athena, I apologize for giving you a hard time. Athena then said: I had to protect you. I contracted with you. You have not been bad. But I will never be a spirit guide for anyone again. I just do not like doing it. It is an ongoing job. It is a big responsibility. You contract to be with the one on earth and help them work through things and get on and stay on the right path.

Next, I dreamed something about an inverted bucket covering a camera.

Interpretation 12/21/2007: Things that are to be revealed to you in life are being hidden. The camera represents pictures and the bucket over the camera means that the things to be revealed are kept from you. Athena says that the bucket symbolizes your life when you had the concussion and near-death-experience. When you returned from that, you were gifted. In this dream, you were working back through your life, reviewing things.

On 11/21/2007, I dreamed that I was with a rather large group of women preparing to speak out for peace, no more wars. I recall the colors of red and white.

Later, again I was with a group of women. This time I estimate five or ten were present. We seemed to be in a park. We wore shorts and shirts. I felt that we were near a beach but I did not see water. I do not know what I looked like. Most of the women appeared to be mid to late forties and energetic. We all seemed to be just traveling without a goal or destination.

Near the end of the dream, a group of men came. I felt that the men came for a purpose. I felt they were musicians in a Rock music band. Then I noticed that one of the women had tattoos. She was wearing a two-piece bathing suit. She and a man walked off together. The other men seemed busy preparing for a concert or something.

Interpretation 12/21/2007: Naomi said, you Spirit Guide is helping me with some of these. This was the Riviera in France. This is one of the lives that you are now living. This is one of your extensions.

You recalled being there. You were there. The men that approached are performers. You and all the women present are married to the members of the band. I said that is exactly what I thought in the dream.

Athena: You are going back into years ago and bringing it forward and you are seeing life extensions that you are living now. *You are living several lifetimes at once.* You are now seeing them and this is to connect with you the cell memory that you are going to be writing about in a book.

The cell memory is brought into the soul from many different lives: the extended lives you lived; the many events that happened in all those lives; and the events that you are aware of in this body. All of it is connected to cell memory. All the cell memory of the soul, a soul, is in the extensions. All of the cell memory of Grace is also in the extended souls of Grace.

This is something that has not been brought to the surface before. Suppose that, in another life, a person died in a cave or a cave in. The soul will carry this event as cell memory. Now, the cell memory may be cleared in the clearing chambers after death. If it is not cleared, it may be carried as claustrophobia in another life. If the person is alive at present, the cell memory may manifest in this life. This is just an example.

Claustrophobic symptoms may manifest within the present you, or within one of the other soul extensions. *It depends on if that cell memory is present in the extension and if an event occurs that triggers the cell memory.* It all depends upon the extension's soul growth and whether the soul brought forth with it that cell memory when it entered the current body. Also, if the cell memory was brought forth, it is more likely to surface in circumstances similar to the first event—for example, the soul is in a human form, and in a similar situation—such as a cave.

Athena: The soul is the soul—a unit—it is just one soul but it splits. The splitting picks up different cell memories from different lives

85

that they have lived. Not just you, but all of the extensions. (Each extension lives a separate life and has cell memories.) This complicates it but I feel you need to know this today. This is something that has to be explored and put into the book.

It has to be examined, accepted and put into a simple form so that it can be accepted. More will be given. That is the purpose of your having dreamed all of those dreams that night so that I, Athena, could come and explain them.

I said this is how I understand the soul—when Creator made each soul, he started with one of his own cells—and this cell contained cell memory. Our soul continues to grow and develop spiritually as long it remains connected to the White Light. I had trouble understanding the "soul splintering" even though it was explained repeatedly by Elijah. He used the octopus as an example—the body symbolized the soul and its tentacles the soul's extensions. The extensions extend out, experience different things and each one brings things back to the whole body. Our soul extensions or splinters do a similar thing. Later, Oshinbah explained it and I finally grasped the idea.

Oshinbah used an orange as a symbol of the soul and how it splits. Picture a whole orange—the rind is the outer wall. It retains and protects the fruit within it. It holds a group of orange wedges in place. Within that rind, each orange wedge is the same. Each wedge of this orange represents a "splinter" of the whole soul.

(The following is an excerpt of the explanation on soul splintering given by Oshinbah on 10/23/2005. This is "As your friend Elijah once elaborated on, being compared to the octopus—the having of many prongs extending out of a major seed. This is as bodies or our spirits are permitted to do in the advanced state we are in—which Earth is not.

It is not that we just go into someone else's body. It is that *we are living many lives at one time.* This has been explained really, really great by your friend Elijah. Only now, we are expanding on it in a different aspect. That aspect is the fact that the galaxy consists of many systems and subsystems of different moons, different suns, different planets revolving around, just as your Earth does among its system.

In doing this, in the galaxy, there will be five to ten—no more than ten—five to ten different lives—as this major component that we have as a spirit. Consider it as an orange. And, the orange if you should slice it or peel it and pull away each slice, therefore, that is the substance of the soul in the galaxy. It can be in these bodies (each slice) living, performing, existing and learning at the same time. When the souls finish their job and exit these physical bodies—or if these five and these five are sleeping or these two and these five and these three are sleeping or doing astral travel—we reunite as the whole orange. The orange is still whole, and as it is divided, what exists is still part of the whole. I believe this will explain to you in a simplified form of what I am speaking.

Also, realize these different forms—in the different galaxies, on Earth, on other planets or wherever they might be—are still learning their unique lessons that each has come to experience. And as they learn and grow spiritually, it in return refurbishes the whole—giving it more of the spiritual—allowing it to grow in the spiritual, and allowing it to accelerate to the head—to the One you know as God—the Supreme Being—the Creator. Now, this may seem complicated to you, you have experienced this my dear. You have done this.

When you come back to the simple life on Earth, as it exists, there can be no recall of this. It would totally do what we call "an overload of your system" and you would be in a mental incapacity and not perform, as even an earthling. Therefore, no recall is allowed to those who experience life on the Earth system. I feel that, having explained the orange concept—I used the fruit—the orange, because it can easily be sliced away and taken away into sections. That explains how the whole is—and the sections return—making the whole even stronger, and even firmer, and more consistent with the Supreme Being.

I do know that this is hard to accept and understand but this is the simplest way that I can explain this to you. To elaborate further on *the intelligence of each of these*—we shall call units—each of these units has its own intelligent quotient depending upon the environment they are in at the time where they are. The main purpose of each of these souls—before it comes back into the whole picture—is to learn the lessons that they need to learn so that they can learn and grow spiritually and advance spiritually and grow spiritually into the wholeness that is of the Creator. By using the orange method—the unit method—you diversify and learn at a faster pace and have more opportunities to accelerate and therefore become completeness with the One—the Creator). End

Back to Dreams

Before the above excerpt on soul splintering, Athena and I were discussing dreams I recorded on 11/21/2007 and she was interpreting them 12/21/2007.

On 12/20/2007, I again thought that we are part of some giant experiment or project, a test or whatever it is. It has many layers whatever it is. Mine is a small but important piece.

Interpreted by Athena12/21/2007: You were on the right course but not about the information you received. What your are speaking of is that we are all part of the big plan, in that we are all particles of Him, of the Creator and, as particles of Him, we are part of a big plan and there are layers, meaning many lifetimes that you exist until you become perfection. When that happens, you are absorbed into the Creator.

To confuse matters even more, I will go ahead, as I am speaking with you, and tell you that those who are evil, who chose to be evil, the ones Naomi calls the Dark Side, they will be absorbed also into the Creator but they will be purified before they are. Do not think that they will enter the Creator and cause a disturbance. This will not be. The Dark will not be cleansed and received back until they ask God to be received and are cleansed. Once they are received, they will be absorbed into the Creatorship, and again, all of us are composed of the Creator. We are particles of the Creator.

This will confuse and frustrate many people especially those who are of religions. This is how it occurs. This is how we were formed. This is how planetary systems were made. *Our Creator did make those. However, the difference in the Creator forming planetary systems and galaxies, and forming humans or souls, is that particles of the Creator Himself are within us. The planetary systems and galaxies are just items he made. The Creator takes a cell from Himself and makes others. That is what he did with souls and that is how we are a part of Him. Also, souls are very elastic, meaning that they can bend and be pulled this way and that or split and have many different lives at the same time.*

Athena: Try not to let this magnify into a mystery or confusion for you. *All is energy. Souls are energy.* That is why the field of technology now developing here on Earth is of pure energy. *The children coming onto Earth that are so brilliant are aligned with this energy* more so than those of you at this time. It is not that they are more of God or less of God. It is the energy itself. The new ones coming onto Earth are more aligned with that energy than you and that's why they demand respect. They feel that their souls are much older and they do not understand the role of parents trying to tell them what to do. However, that is a problem they need to adjust to. They do not need to overrule the parents. That is their lesson that they came to learn. The lesson is that no matter the age, experience, or how much energy you have, once you are with others you learn to be respectful. *You do not use what you have, as a means of control.*

And even with the advanced technology and knowledge they have when they come onto earth, they too have come to learn a lesson. *Their lesson is obedience and learning to be patient with those who do not have the abilities that they have. None of you are on Earth without a purpose. The whole is to learn to work with each other and to know that each of us is here to perfect a little more.* I don't mean to preach to you but these are explanations that I felt we needed to discuss.

Dreams

On 11/23/2007, I was awake about three o'clock and had trouble sleeping. Then later, I awoke after having a series of dreams about being with a black man and black woman at different sites. The woman and I were together the first time we saw the man. We did not seem to know each other. The man and woman were very serious. The second time we met, she and I went to a room where he was. The third time we were together we were outside. Someone was directing one of them on how to walk down a "stage-ramp." It made me think of preparation for a performance, maybe a play. I do not know if I was black and I do not know the nationality of the people. We all seemed of medium height and weight.

The only other thing I recall was that in the middle of the night, I dreamed of the same sentence said to me twice but it seemed very insignificant and I can't recall it.

Interpreted 12/21/2007 by Athena: Black and white—symbolizes the balancing of life. *You were awake between the hours of three and four and that is when you have the highest opportunity of connecting with the Creator.* So, after you awoke and returned to sleep you were given knowledge of what you were trying to reach on the spiritual side. This is what these dreams approaching will discuss. Now, proceed and excuse me for interrupting.

The sentence said to you was not insignificant but it was not planned for you to recall what was said to you. It was meant for the soul. It was meant for the soul to digest. Your soul received it. Your soul dealt with it.

Now, back to the black man and black woman—that shows perfect balance, the same color and would be so if both were yellow or white—that shows perfection. You, in the dream, being white with the black shows balance—even though you had two black and one white and then it intermingled—it showed that you can still be centered in God and that is what you were doing. The platform you described and the proper walking was the walk of life to help each other and give each other instructions on the walk or path of life. That is what this was about.

Very few understand dream symbols. Unless you are a trained soul from the Other Side, you never really grasp what the dream is about. Naomi is one who is gifted in interpreting dreams. This soul has had many lifetimes of this profession on Earth and on other planets.

The dream state is more prevalent on Earth. Dreams are the way humans work through their daily problems. Some dreams have no meaning. But the dreams that you are having are deliberately given through the spirit. That is because of your conquest of the spiritual path that you are on. I will continue to help you with this. Now, I will allow you to finish your dreams.

On 11/24/2007, I dreamed several things during the night but the following is all I recall. I was riding in a car with someone. We were on a road and I noticed a house. The house was set back from the road. Actually, it was sitting in a field. The house was two stories tall and had gables and windows along the roofline.

The issue in the dream was venting the house by opening the windows and whether the windows of the house were presently open or closed. I felt that if they windows were open and it rained, the rain might go into the house. The house seemed rather plain. I did not see any shrubs or flowers. I don't know who owned the house. I think I lived there.

Interpreted by Athena 12/21/2007. My dear, the vehicle and the house represent you. The vehicle of course is your soul and the house is your spiritual growth. So, the house that you were observing and felt the windows needed to be open, that is correct, you do. Your soul needs to vent and yet, you are frightened to vent. If you open up and vent you fear that substances (humans) may throw water on your spiritual growth. However, you received in your dream state the necessity to vent anyway. Your dream is telling you to speak out. Even though you feel this way, speak out and let your spiritual self grow. You have grown anyway, and past that. The dream simply said vent, even though the rain might fall on you, vent.

The next dream I had was that someone spoke of a person who is over 90 years old. The person needs to cleanse before crossing over. I did not get a name but I think it was my mother-in-law Dot, because she was the first one I thought of when I woke up. Athena confirmed that I was accurate. She went on to give reassurance that this soul would be cleansed to some degree before she crosses and that she has much debriefing to do.

On 11/25/2007, I dreamed that I was about age 35 and female. I was rushing to catch a train. The train station was on top of a hill and I was down the hill in a building. People were helping me get things together to catch the train. It seemed important that I catch the train. I was wearing a suit but no topcoat. It was very cold outside and there was snow and ice all over the ground and very slippery. A policeman helped me up the icy hill by letting me hold onto his arm.

Interpretation 12/21/2007. One of authority will assist you. However, this was in the country of the frozen ice, a life that you are now living. In the dream state, you are going into the different lives you are living. You will be assisted by a higher authority—the police officer in the dream represents those of the Other Side helping you. The train is just a matter of transportation, again your vehicle.

That life that you are now living is very slippery. It is very unstable, unsure at this time. So, one of higher authority—me, your spirit guide in that life also—is assisting you so that your life will not be so skittish, slippery and unstable. I will be helping with you.

I asked Athena: What is the problem? She replied: It is a lifetime that you chose to work through some problems. But, you are unsure if you are doing the right thing or not. We, on the Other Side, are assisting you in this. I asked what country and she said Russia.

I continued speaking of the dreams from 11/25/2007. Someone said a coat would be at the station for me. I thought of a beige coat with a belt and fur collar. It was about size ten. I got to the station and looked in a storage closet for coats but did not see the coat. I thought someone might have taken it because it was a nice coat. I was trying to decide whether to continue the trip without the coat and take the chance or I turn back. I was inclined to turn back but I awoke.

Interpretation by Athena 12/21/2007: The rest of the dream is about your journey in that life in Russia. You had found this life so difficult that your soul—the coat represents the human body—was trying to determine whether it should return back home or go on in the human life. You will continue. We have walked you through that. To return would be of no avail.

About 3:50 a.m., I dreamed that I was in an area with very bright lights. I dreamed something about a stainless steel cart on wheels. It had several shelves which contained something that I thought was fruits and vegetables. I think I started to get up and go get the cart but instead, I asked someone to bring the cart to me.

Interpretation by Athena 12/21/2007: *Stainless steel means that there is strength* in what you are dealing with. Steel represents one of the hardened materials of life that you cannot destroy. What you have in your life that is going on now has an array of functions and what your mission is will not be destroyed.

Later, I had a separate dream of lying on my left side in my bed and receiving help with my physical self. I started to feel sensations along the left hip, leg, and foot. Also, my left arm and hand ached at intervals.

Athena said: This was an actual healing. I did this. I am not a physical healer. Those of the Other Side who are healers came forth to assist you.

Next, I had a very involved and detailed dream but I do not recall that much of it. I was doing serious work making a mold and castings from the mold. I don't know what the object was that I was making but it seemed important. I felt that it had something to do with a repair of a piece of equipment outside the building in the driveway. I do not know what but it was clear at the time.

Interpretation by Athena 12/21/2007: The molds and castings are the touching of lives that you will be doing with the books that you are writing and presenting to the public. You are affecting and influencing many, many souls on Earth. That is the mold and casting. The outside—where you speaking of something being repaired outside of your home—that is the message—souls being repaired outside of your home.

At seven o'clock, I awoke. I had dreamed I was a teenage girl. I had a nice boyfriend and a nice mother. The boy and I had been separated briefly but we knew it was temporary we were still in the same room. The woman smiled. The boy came close and sat beside me. I combed his hair. I am not sure the color of his hair. At first, I thought blonde but then it seemed dark brown.

Interpretation by Athena 12/21/2007: This was a very short life you had in Ireland. This is a previous life of joy and happiness. You took care of this boy. Your mother was a wonderful soul. The color of the hair was red. The year was around 823 A.D. The country was not known as Ireland at that time.

On 11/26/2007, I woke up about 2:00 a.m. I had dreamed of a young man about age 30 who appeared wearing dark dress trousers with a fine yellow line that created a design in the trousers. He wore a leather bomber style jacket that was dark golden tan, unusual color not brown and tan. The jacket had a patina that caught the light. Also, the cuffs and bottom of the jacket were knit cuffs I believe that is all I recall. I don't know who the man was or what he looked like. The coat looked like it was heavy and built for rugged cold weather.

Interpretation by Athena 12/21/2007: That was a pilot during WWII who was actually shot down. It was someone your father knew. It was a bomber jacket, the kind worn when the bombs were dropped on Hiroshima. He was not shot down at that time. He was an acquaintance of your father. They lived in the same county. The pilot later moved to your present area. You were small when he died. He didn't drop bombs but he did pilot the planes. You can search your area for names of pilots of WWII. It is a common name like Clement, Dixon, Smith, or Rogers. These are names on the list that went together. Clement was the first name given by Athena when you asked.

About 6:00 a.m. on 11/26/2007, I dreamed that I was with two other women in what appeared to be a thrift shop. We were picking up sweaters and checking them for defects and quality. I found one sweater and thought that one looks like mine. It had a large hole in it.

Next, I was in a small room that for some reason, I thought was Vicki's bedroom. I looked under the bed and to my surprise it was lit up completely. Another smaller bed appeared under her bed. On top of this bed was a pair of my pajamas with blue and white stripes. I said to Vicki, the next time you're in your room, please go under the bed and get my pajamas for me.

Interpretation by Athena: You'll be asking Vicki for assistance. The bed is a place of rest. Vicki is supposed to be assisting you with the books and give you the rest and assurance you need on the books. You were asking her in your dream to give you the aid you need so that you can rest. The different bed underneath her bed, indicates more than one person involved in this project. The hole in the garment means the project is incomplete. Vicki is not participating at this point.

Next, I was outside standing at the top of a long hill. There was a road up the hill and a fence between where I was and the road. There was a path on the side where I was. A man was walking up the hill toward me. He had a large white drink container in his hand. When he reached me, he wanted me to finish the drink. It was a cream colored liquid and I drank it. In the bottom of the container I saw a maraschino cherry and a few small green stems. He gave me the cherry and wanted me to eat it. I did. The man seemed familiar. I thought he might be the Polynesian man I recently dreamed about.

Interpretation by Athena: You are on your path. Cherry represents the fruit of life. You were being offered the chalice or the representation of life—the life being fruitful. The man on the path was not your husband in your life this time. It was a soul representing the Master. The soul was offering you the chalice of life—the bread of life—you took it graciously. You were on your own path. This soul came into your path to give to your soul that which is life—life more abundantly—life that is more fruitful. They were letting you know that in this life you are doing what you came here to do.

It was actually the Master. He came in disguise. We call him Jesus. The Christ that we know on Earth is a Divine Master, one that is very elevated and next to the Creator and he can take any form that he wishes. His main point was to give unto you the knowledge of the fruitfulness of life and that you are on the path that evolves you. This is a high honor.

On 11/27/2007, I awoke at 12:00 midnight. I had dreamed that I was outside standing near a table. A two-story clapboard house was nearby. A man was to my right and a woman to my left. I think we all were black. I was serving meat and potatoes to these two people. The man commented that I did not serve him the potato or meatball he wanted. I realized that he was kidding. He was complimenting the food and making sure that he got every morsel possible. He was teasing me. The tone was one of fun, food and happiness sharing the food. I knew them well.

Interpretation by Athena: This setting was like a plantation in Africa. It was an African life you had. You were like a servant in the house and the couple thought of you as their child although you were not at the time. The man liked to tease you like that because you would take him seriously and then he would get a big laugh. This is not an extension but another life. The master of the house delighted in you, as though you were his child. Actually, Athena says that in other lives, you have been his child and that is why the closeness was felt.

On 11/28/2007, I woke up at 11:45 p.m. following a dream. My recall was vague once I was out of bed. The dream was about an experiment with cell memory. Someone was with me. The person had also done work with cell memory, and wrote of it, as I am doing. The person had worked at the same site with the same family and expressed having experienced trouble with the family when the publication of the material was due. I responded that so far, mine has been okay. But as I read the note this morning, I thought, I have nothing published yet.

Interpretation by Naomi 1/4/2008: The cell memory book will be published but you had the dream to let you know that it will be a struggle to get it published. Also, I am being told that the person that came to you in the dream about the trouble he had with getting the cell memory information published, this person is deceased. The person is assisting you so that you do not have to go through this.

In a dream on 11/28/2007, I recommended someone named Gonzales as being nice. I said that in cooking school, he would let us leave our experiments there for two hours. I woke up and when I returned to bed, I dreamed the same thing again.

Interpretation by Naomi 1/4/2008: This dream is telling you that you will find someone foreign that is trustworthy enough for you to recommend. The person will also befriend you. He is someone you do not know yet.

Around 3:30 a.m. 11/29 I awoke following this dream. I was with two female children. One was about age 12 and one was a young teen. These kids seemed street wise. One told me she planned to go to N. J. by train after school to register for a class and then return by train thereafter. The other girl said something about needing another pair of shoes or sneakers. I saw that she wore high top white sneakers. She seemed to be in the aisle of a store as she spoke. I think the two girls planned to travel together. My main concern was the time of travel. Part of the trip would be after dark. I considered their present school hours and the hours of the school in New Jersey where they intended to go. I thought that is the only option. The schools are not open weekends. The communication was by thought. I also had an image of a gray colored wall or a large gray flat surface in front of me at some point. I woke up.

Interpretation by Naomi 1/4/2008: This is about the youth of that area not having a solid foundation to stand on. Shoes symbolize foundation.

Your concern was their being out after dark but the issue is they don't have a foundation to stand on and travel at anytime is dangerous. The youth of today often lack balance and a strong foundation.

On 11/29/2007 11:30 p.m. I woke up. I had dreamed of what I believe to be a cell memory cleansing ceremony or preparation for something related to it. There was someone with me, probably Athena, although, I did not see anyone. I talked with someone by thought. There was a round bowl about 6 inches in diameter. There was a rectangular dish maybe ten by twelve inches. There was a question of which container to use. I chose the round bowl. Someone said to me, do not be surprised at anything that is said by this individual because the individual is unaware of what is occurring at present. Be careful whom you trust with the material.

Interpretation by Athena 1/4/2008: Athena is laughing. Have you noticed a lot more is occurring about cell memory? And, it is centering you on cell memory and getting it accomplished. You were on the Other Side. The different bowls tell you that you will have different choices on how to receive and present the materials. You were cautioned. Some people may appear to be trustworthy and not be. The objects of how to prepare, you chose the right one but that was symbolic. It means there will be different opportunities to get your material.

Later in the night, I dreamed of being with a group of women. We were sitting and discussing with someone what things we can now physically do at the age we are. The lady beside me was older and could do less than I could. The person taking the information seemed younger than others in the room.

Next, I dreamed that another person and I were getting physical therapy. We each were lying on our backs on treatment tables, which were in a straight-line single file. A woman was positioned with the top of her head toward the soles of my feet. Someone told each of us our treatment schedules and what would be treated. I do not recall the schedules, they were detailed and I felt like the therapist might alternate between us, that is, treat her then me.

Interpretation by Athena 1/4/2007: You were at different levels spiritually. This is saying to you that no matter the age of the physical body, it must be taken care of. Whatever the body needs, it must be taken care of because it is the temple for the soul. The human body, according to the Holy Scriptures is a holy temple that belongs to God. Therefore, no matter the age of the body, it must be nourished. The physical therapy was to let the body prepare and be nurtured.

11/30/2007. File 30145. Reflexology Session

I told Naomi of my dreams. We are trying to get all the dreams interpreted.

On 11/30/2007, I had a dream around midnight and then woke up. There was an open truck bed loaded with something like green sorghum canes. I was walking and running trying to catch up with the truck.

Interpretation by Naomi on 1/4/2007: Vehicles are your body. Sugar Cane or Sorghum means nourishment and you are seeking nourishment. The vehicle means you were watching your own body try to get the nourishment it needs. When you see food, especially green food, this represents nourishment to your spirit/soul.

This morning, 1/4/2007, I woke up to record this dream at 5:15. I was in a hotel room alone. I was traveling. My clothes were neatly hung in my closet. Then I went outside. It was sunny. I went somewhere but things started to go wrong. I was at a place to catch transportation somewhere and realized suddenly that I had no purse, no money and no luggage. I was confused as to what was happening.

Next, I don't know what life this was or what location. My husband and I were with another man and woman on a patio. The other man was tall and thin. I said to my husband it is 12:30 and we should go. He said no. The clock is wrong. It is 1:30. Then it was 2:30. The other woman was small in stature. She was lying on her left side with her face to the back of a loveseat. Two people could have sat there. My husband was lying on his left side in spoon position behind her. He started kissing or nibbling her right ear. The other man was standing. I was sitting. I don't know what I looked like. I got up and bent over my husband and tried to bite his ear. At this point, I started to wake up. I wondered why I was doing this. I remember thinking, detach from this. The ear suggests listen to me, hear me. This is a learning situation, which has been given.

I said to Naomi I think a lot of the dreaming is cell memory being brought up in dreams. I am supposed to bring them to the surface and clear them. Learning to clear cell memories is one of the reasons I came to Earth this time. When I am on the Other Side, one of my jobs is to work with the most difficult cases and help them clear cell memory.

I feel that this is a time that both my husband and I have things we are experiencing and wading through. We are working through things and clearing in order to develop spiritually. I hope someone today will explain this dream. Naomi acted like I had not spoken anything. She was staring off to the right and suddenly said someone is here and started to channel Dr. Freud.

Dr. Freud

Interpretation by Dr. Freud 1/4/2007: We were not eavesdropping, we don't do that but we are aware of all that happens on Earth. We are aware of what you were speaking about earlier. The dreams were discussed to a certain extent. The party that is doing the cell memory work, who spoke of the dreams, one thing I would like to clarify with her is that the dream you thought was a dream was a reality. I asked which dream he meant.

Dr. Freud replied, the one you spoke of with the other female in it. (He did not elaborate). As you stated when you came into this room, there is not enough time to discuss all the dreams you have had. As you said, it would take a week of consistent work.

But how obedient you have been unto my requests that I made of you. I applaud you. You are the most excellent of students. I greatly admire your dedication in this endeavor you pursue. I applaud you. You are doing such a great job that my assistants or helpers have been of little use to you. You are doing it on your own. Forget that I am Dr. Freud. This would come from anyone that has observed you. Your dedication has led you into the many, many dream states that you have had. Let me explain to you, as a professional person, many of these dreams are helping you work through many of your personal problems. It is to get you past the personal problems so that you can dedicate one hundred percent toward the cell memory and the work you are doing in that area.

To get the total dedication, you have to get the garbage out of the way. You have to work through it and that is what a lot of the dreams are about. This is so that you can get the garbage out. Once you get the garbage out, things will flow smoothly. And it already is coming along very nicely.

A lot of the garbage, as you know, has to do with the husband and the many prior lives you have had together—and the lives with each other that you never finished your mission—the emotional part, which in your life right now—is intermingling. The human emotional part is intermingling with the soul of you that is dedicated to doing the cell memory work.

Now, I am assisting you in clearing out the garbage. This is why you are having more dreams than we anticipated that you would. It will be a big task for this person Naomi. But once you have the dreams typed, I ask that you present them to Naomi for her to briefly analyze. She elaborates too much. Present at least five dreams per session, when you first come in, until all are dealt with. I ask this because she is gifted in explaining dream states. Also, she is sensitive and clairvoyant. She not only interprets the dreams but she also knows when the dreams are interrelating to other aspects of life. She does not beat around and avoid issues but speaks plainly. Bring at least five dreams per session. Five is a symbol of completeness for her.

You have been able to determine the purpose and meanings of some dreams but I am requesting that we put it on record and have another individual look at it. Some of your interpretations are a little wavy and we need clarification on it. With your consent, I would like this to be done.

Dr. Freud continued, now the dreams that I told you that you would encounter, so that you may learn, prepare, and be ready for the cell memory book, these have been completed and we will let up on those at night. You will not have as many. Now the dream state is very beneficial so I am not saying they will cease. I am saying the number of dreams will decrease to two or three.

While you are visiting in the area of your vacation, we desire that you not experience dreams of this manner while you are there. We want you to have a total vacation and not go and have dreams that you have to be concerned about, write down, and wonder what they mean. If you do have dreams that you feel are strong or have a purpose, write them. If you dream, while away on vacation, they may be silly dreams because of where you are and spending time with loved ones. Do you have any questions for me?

I answered that I do have questions but I am not sure how to ask them. *Dr. Freud said,* just speak what is in the heart. I said, okay. The dream that I had this morning that I spoke about, in the first part of the dream, I had no wallet, and no luggage. And, from this one, I went into the dream about my husband and a female lying in spoon position with the female and kissing her right ear or whatever he was doing. I want to know what this was about.

Dr. Freud: You are asking me for clarification of what this was about? I answered yes. Please explain this. Dr. Freud explained that the first part of the dream of losing the wallet and other items are symbols in the dream state. A wallet represents material things—papers are stored there. The losing of those is showing you introspection—the losing of personal items is necessary at times to feel what the soul feels. We do not mean that in actuality that you will lose them. What we are stating is that you will lose the desire to have those—as much as you will desire to have the cell memory revealed to you and to pursue this.

In other words, what you feel is of importance, or what humans value as of importance are symbolized—as in wallets, papers, jewelry, clothes—are of no importance. Because, you went straight from that into what does bother you. What is concerning you and is trying—let me also interject at this point that the Dark Entities on the earth will take any means whatsoever to slow down progress in the earth's ascension—especially dedicated souls such as yourself. There is a negative side to all of us, while we are on earth. The negative side of your life has been explained to you before. That was interjected in your dream state that was coming from the Other Side—from where we are—of the importance of staying on your path and to allow the materialistic things to disappear. If they do disappear, just focus on what you are here for.

At that point, the Dark Entities interjected the scene that they knew would disturb you, that of the husband in the spoon position, and they drew a clear picture in the mind of what was happening. In other words, picture a book that you are reading and we are telling you of the ways that you will be accelerating you growth in learning of the cell memory, and the next few pages would give you a lot more information. But, instead of those pages, the Dark Forces have replaced those with their vision, and their version of what is going on in your life, as a human. It has no bearing whatsoever, on the cell memory. It was a Dark Entity, or in this case, more than one Dark Entity, that revived a fear or this past life memory of the spouse that you now have and his infidelities. This interferes with the present human side of you. So, be aware of the power that the Dark Side has. They are good at this. They try to stop, slow down, delay, or actually do away with anything prospering the soul. You are prospering the soul with the cell memory work.

I verified what I had heard. So, they can come through in dreams and do this kind of thing?

Dr. Freud answered yes. They can and do commit such acts. Could we stop it on this side? Yes. But, let me explain: You or rather, your soul is learning to avoid this. We allow the interjection from this side. We allow it so that your soul may learn what is happening, what is occurring. When the soul learns or recognizes what is occurring or has occurred, then the soul states to the human body: This is of no importance. This is of the past, so let go. It has been cleared. Once this is done, the Dark Entities have no power. They cannot interject that which you will not receive. Does this explain it to you? I answered yes. But I have been told events will continue to happen.

Dr. Freud said: Events will keep happening until you have grown to the physical point, which is perfection and this does not occur on Earth. So, yes, they will continue. I am just explaining to you today why you received that, when you were being given other information.

I do appreciate your asking things, which are of a bothersome nature to you. At times, the messages will be sent to your husband while you are here. And, as happened this week, messages will be sent to you while he is here. This is because both of you are growing spiritually and you both are able to accept this at this point. This is like when Elijah was here when your husband was here this week, he desired for you to have a message and told your husband. So, from the Other Side, as we are frequently called, you will receive these in the dream state, and actually, while you are consciously awake. *It is not a test. It is just allowing you to develop in other areas.* Some will be of importance to be delivered to him. He will also begin receiving these. Allow him to hear or read this message.

Messages given to you in the waking state will occasionally pertain to your husband. Give them to him whether he acknowledges them or not. Give the messages to him. We are giving a directive to you: You will be allowed to give information to him that we give or that your spirit guide will help you in your training. Also, explain to him that this is a spiritual growth pattern. This will allow him to grow spiritually, to learn in the human form, to accept that which is given in this direction. This is a training session.

I responded that I recall what has been channeled in other sessions about cell memory clearing. Both my husband and I have experienced a lot in this and other lifetimes. We each must clear these cell memories to grow spiritually. Clearing cell memory is easier to accomplish while on this side.

As I understand it, I charted before coming here to experience these things. The goal was to return to the Other Side and be able to help souls clear cell memories. Clearing the most difficult cases was a job I was given. I feel that I am not stating this clearly.

Dr. Freud said no, it is very clear. The soul's perfection continues to work when you arrive on the Other Side and apply the knowledge and information that you gained while you were here on Earth. The soul has to grow like that. It is the soul's evolution and you are right on target with that. No two souls are alike.

Your souls have been intertwined for so many lifetimes, especially in the Earth sphere, and as stated before by others, Earth is a school. That is why you are here. You each have had dynamic and challenging life experiences. Many of these experiences were negative. You chose to work through these, which allows great spiritual growth. The challenges you diagrammed and placed in your charts, before you came on Earth, were deliberate acts so that you could grow at that deliberate speed on the soul evolution.

The two of you undertook tremendous soul lives on Earth, of such dimension, that many would have found impossible. But you two were adequately prepared and had done your homework on this side. You were adequately advised and knew exactly what you were coming into.

Both of you are back on track. There was a delay in the New York life when neither of you had entered the spiritual field at this depth. The husband has been much slower on his path. You have helped him tremendously. Although, you have been hindered, with a noose around your neck, by all the past life experiences that you have carried with you, the insecurities of his enjoyment of the feminine, and the back and forth with the two of you. That is what you chose, so that you could overcome that and be the wonderful soul when you do arrive back here. As complicated as it seems, it is very simple. This is an Earth thing you are dealing with. When you are over here, the Earth thing is gone.

When you return to the Other Side, you have access to your own record. You are debriefed. You will know and see how you have grown. You will have clearance and all of this garbage will be thrown out. The soul will be purified to the degree that it has evolved and there will be nothing at all of the remnants of the past lives, the jealousy, the insecurities and all that. Those are emotions experienced on Earth. On this side is total love and total happiness.

I do hope this has helped you. I too must return to my classroom. I will still be working with you and I will give you the Earth timeframe. The Earth timeframe, from this coming week, Wednesday, from that day until the fifteenth of December, we will do no homework. I will not be coming to your area until after the 15th. That is to give your brain a rest and forget us over here.

Keep in mind always, this parting thought: The experiences on earth are unique to Earth. No other place has the emotional state and the fast method of soul evolution as the planet Earth does. So, as trying as the experiences on Earth are, the rewards are immense. To grow, you have to have the turmoil, the experiences and the negative that you can reject. Consider being on Earth as a choice that you made so that you and other souls could grow at a rapid rate. I must say farewell.

Dreams

On 12/1/2007 around 2 a.m., I dreamed that my husband and I attended a gathering of very intelligent people. They were club members. I saw two lines of people. They walked single file in opposite directions. They were all neatly dressed in modern clothes. They walked uphill in a straight line and then downhill. For some reason, I thought of a funeral. I never saw a body, nor did anyone say anything. One or two people felt familiar but I am not sure who they were. The area was heavily wooded and I felt like we were walking on manmade paths—maybe in a park—just wide enough for two people to pass each other.

Interpretation by Naomi 1/4/2008: I am getting information. This is showing you that this group is so structured that they are like robots. They have knowledge and capacities beyond what you could describe but they don't have feelings.

Later, I dreamed that we were with two men from the club. I knew one of the men but not the other. We were inside a restaurant. At one point, I read a memo a woman had left. At some point, I saw a typed Tellers Check.

Then I went outside a little earlier ahead the men and the same woman passed and handed me another note and this was essentially the same as the first but it had been altered. One area was obliterated and a hand written note inserted. Then, the men came out. I commented to the men that the woman had left another note. But now, the woman looked totally different. She went from an appearance of high energy, neat and intelligent, to trashy and dirty and she had a child with her. She and the child got into a dirty, beat-up, red car.

The two men got into the front seat of a car. We got into the back seat. The man we did not know was the driver. The other man was a passenger. We were happy and laughing. At some point the men in the front seat were naked. I don't know how it happened. Then we all were suddenly out of the car and standing. The driver of the car was laughing so hard that he sat on the ground in the yoga position of Child's Pose and rocked to and fro with laughter. The other man was hysterical laughing and naked also. We were dressed and not concerned with this.

At one point, the man we knew had soft white fabric bags partially filled with something, maybe sand or flour. The bags were shaped like pendulous breasts. He taped several of these onto areas of his body: his chest, his back and his crotch. Somehow, we ended up at a house that felt like ours. We all went inside. The two men were socializing in one room. We were in a different room and my husband was affectionate. I don't recall this happening before.

Interpretation by Naomi 1/4/2008: The waitress person was symbolic of the members in that club. They are one-way at a meeting but totally different when they leave. They are not what they appear to be at the meeting in other words. Their appearance is highly altered when they leave the meeting.

With the man you knew, if you saw the man as he truly is, you would see that he carries a great deal of baggage. The areas that he had the bags placed are important. He was trying to maintain balance. The dream said: If you actually saw me as I am, you would see my baggage.

Later, I dreamed of two memo-sized pieces of paper. I read the papers while they were on a table. I think they were about diets: the diet one on the right was regular; the diet on the left was a special problem diet with a black arc on it. The second time I saw these two pieces of paper I was holding them in my hand. I held the special problem diet in my left hand. Jean, my sister, grabbed it from me and said I need this one.

On 12/2/2007, I dreamed of a large room, which seemed separate from the main house. I went to the room. Young boys, maybe teens were there doing self-destructive behaviors, but I am not sure what. I think it was taking drugs or something. They were just acting a silly and doing dumb things like diving onto beds and then onto the floor. I did not approve of their behavior. They left the room and a man came into the room. We changed the pillowcases on the beds where the boys had been. Things were disheveled. I woke up. Naomi interpreted the dream on 1/4/2008: Possibly, the dream represents confusion with youth. You changed the pillowcases so that their acts did not affect you. Pillows suggest a place to rest your head and think clearly.

Later, I dreamed of being in a bed wearing a shirt and underwear. I was lying on my back talking to a man lying to my left side. He also wore a shirt or pajamas and underwear or pajamas bottoms. He was lying on his back. We were talking about something. The man was a friend that I have known since I was about twelve years old.

I said, we had better get up and get dressed, they will be here soon. I just know these things. As soon as I said it, I looked around the room and did not see my pants. I realized the room was cluttered with clothes everywhere. Just then, people came and they seemed to be part of the family. The man was looking for his pants and I recalled he had been wearing navy blue pants. I entered another room and saw more clothes, some hanging and some scattered all over. I dressed and went back. The man was sitting on his feet on the bed wearing gold satin pants.

Interpreted by Naomi 1/4/2008: This disheveled life is exactly how this man's life is at this time. The family structure and anyone of the family connected to them, this is how it is in their lives and you are picking this up.

Next, I dreamed of someone who made coats. A delivery truck filled with coats appeared. Men unloaded the coats and took them into a building. The coats looked complete but someone said the sleeves had to be altered. I woke up and again returned to sleep.

Naomi said this dream has substance. The coat has the function of clothing the soul. In other words, the coats represent the covering of the human body, which covers the soul. The coats being incomplete means there is still work to be done.

Later, I dreamed that I was in a nice house. It was very orderly and had white walls. I really like it. As I woke up I realized it was my house.

On December 3, 2007, I woke up and my mind wandered to the garbage I carry around and how to release it. I realize that part of the garbage is past lives. Part of it is current life issues, which pop up as reminders. What is so annoying is that all seems fine, I relax and start enjoying life and once again, I get blindsided. Enough! No more.

As I lay there, I suddenly realized that I had dreamed before I woke up. I recalled being with Rob and my father. I felt total love pouring onto me from them. At one point, I remember holding Rob's right hand with my left one. My Dad appeared and said by thought "seeing you two together feels normal." I remember when Dad died, Rob said he raced to the funeral home when he learned I was on my way there. He did not want me to be alone when I saw Dad dead. He held my hand my right and stayed with me. I recall that we often did that when either of us was in pain. I feel that these two souls knew I needed to feel love and they came as I slept and gave me love and caring. This was a very nice warm feeling. Today, I have felt better.

Interpretation by Dr. Freud through Naomi 1/4/2008: This was a reality. It was not a dream. It happened. Your father said it feels normal because what you are doing is normal. The two men were saying to you that what you are doing and what you are accomplishing is right. It's normal.

Later, I felt like I was out of body up high and I was looking down. I saw myself, my physical self, standing beside a man on a wide ramp in front of a huge elevated billboard. The billboard color was sky blue except for a white area on the left. The word Iceland was written in huge white capital letters. I felt okay.

Interpretation on 1/4/2008 by Dr. Freud through Naomi: The ice of Iceland is melting at a much faster rate than is made public. The scientists have informed the government but the government does not want to publish this. Iceland will be gone.

On 12/4/2007, I dreamed of a few people in a line at a grocery store. They were talking of the war and finances. I think it is probably the new man who is in charge of the Federal Reserve Bank. The store cashier asked customers if they wanted meat and if the groceries were to be charged. The meat looked like beef. I did not see any money. The tone was a money issue.

Interpretation by Dr. Freud via Naomi: That dream signifies that the one controlling the purse strings is telling the people that they have a choice. They have choices to make about substances to support the physical self. Beef will support more growth but vegetables are also good. The body needs protein. The choice of cash or credit card is a choice that people will have to make, as the economy declines and food is rationed. To give up all credit is a choice they will have to make. To clear out credit cards is a must. The choice of cash or credit card at the cash register will determine whether people get the beef or no beef.

This time is fast approaching. The economy of the United States is a problem. When leaders try to pacify the people by giving them a substance—a little monetary thing, a little bonus, when the country is already trillions of dollars in debt, it is not happening. The Dark Side is so intent on hanging on, they have lost ground totally, but they are trying to persuade the public, and will do anything to get the people to keep on trusting them. The majority of people are not taken in. It is going to get much worse.

On 12/5/2007, I dreamed that I was a passenger in a large truck. Another large truck appeared. The truck paint was yellow with various colored streak across the yellow. Inside the truck were two black men who seemed very menacing. They were trying to intimidate and use the truck for scare tactics.

Interpretation by Naomi 1/4/2008: This is simple. It means that someone or people in your life will use every method possible to derail you from your mission or purpose. They will show themselves to be underhanded and conniving. They represent the Dark Side. The dream is telling you this. Do they need to tell you who they are? No. The dream is just telling you that the men symbolize the Dark Side that will be zeroing in, not only you, but also all who are of the White Light, at this time.

Later, I dreamed that I was inside a building walking toward a conference room where many people were gathered. I entered the room through double doors. Immediately, I saw a small thin woman with dark hair stand up from her seat. She was at a rectangular table that would seat about six people. She wore a black dress. It was unusual in that the top was a heavy thread but open weave knit. The thread used was much was heavier than thread used for lace designs. I approached the woman as if she was a friend and I was glad to see her. She was courteous to me. I do not know who she was. She left. I took her place at the table. I stood for a few minutes but she did not return so I sat down.

Interpretation by Athena via Naomi 1/11/2008: Do your recall her age? I said maybe thirty-five or forty. Athena is laughing and having fun with this one. Athena: You were on the Other Side. There is no time frame. You were in the Hall of Justice. There is a large area there where a spiritual self presides over different things that are brought up on different occasions. This woman got up and relinquished her place so that you could preside over that which was to come.

That is an honor. The position is one you occupy when you are over there and you are over there quite often. You thought it was a dream but it was not. You were actually there so you wrote about it. This is a place of honor and distinction that you occupy. This may be the first you have written about it.

12/28/2007. I dreamed that men were digging in my yard. I do not know the location. I spoke with a man to ask what they were doing. He said we are doing the work you asked for. I objected. They were working and I had not seen any plans or given approval for this. I observed a pile of sod rolled up and a pile of dirt. It was layered according to type of dirt.

Then I was standing inside a room with white walls. The work crew had already excavated a large amount of dirt from the floor. I realized they planned to remove this entire room of dirt and then fill the entire room with new dirt. I said this would cost a fortune and is not necessary and it made now sense. All they needed to do was remove about a foot of topsoil and replace it with good soil. I wanted to see written plans and costs.

The man said the cost was projected at six thousand dollars. This appeared to be reasonable. However, I felt there was an alternate solution. If the entire room is cleared of dirt, leave the room without dirt. A new floor could be installed. A second story could be added on top of this room. Or, where the soil is excavated outside, build a second room there.

Interpretation on 1/4/2007 by Naomi: That was the house you lived in when you were married in N. Y. right? I said yes, I think so. She said: That means the residue of negative events that happened there have returned. The symbol is the dirt being dug up. The seems to be related to your husbands spiritual growth and the opportunity is there to clear and rebuilt, which is symbolized by the white walls. The outcome depends upon how he handles the opportunities that arise.

12/29/2007. I dreamed that my daughter and my husband and I were in a very big corridor. At first, I seemed to be there alone. Then I looked behind me. I saw Vicki. Then my husband arrived and went on ahead. I started to follow him but felt I should wait for Vicki. Eventually, Vicki took another turn and I was alone again. I woke up.

Interpretation 1/11/2008 by Athena and Chief White Cloud: Your husband has gone on in front meaning he has grown a lot spiritually and made a lot of progress. Vicki sat down and then she went through another door. Her soul growth is okay. She took a detour to do other work.

1/1/2008. I had a very detailed dream, which I have condensed. My husband and I entered a military base to shop for furniture. We took different directions to cover more ground quickly. I went in and out of buildings. I measured furniture. I saw a party in progress and people were dancing. I went to building where a party had been. There were many empty cups. Then my husband joined me there and a lady gave him a key to the building where a party had been held.

Interpretation 1/11/2008: Your husband and you are on separate paths but they merge. You work together to achieve the goals for which you came to Earth this time. You're assisting/supportive of his spiritual growth. He came to learn of the emotions and is doing an excellent job. The empty cups you saw will be filled and the key that was given to him is symbolic of the support and guidance he is receiving. He is working hard and will achieve the goals he set for himself.

1/5/2008. I dreamed that my husband and I were driving on a dirt road at the edge of a field. Next to the road and in the distance, there were rolling hills that were unusual in color. They were yellow and some had areas of orange with white small openings. Out of these opening plumes of white smoke rose into the air.

We drove under the limbs of very unusual trees. Their trunks and branches were black and the limbs were long and hung over the road. When we passed under the limbs, white blobs of powder fell onto the vehicle. As I spoke of the dream, Athena, my Spirit Guide, said Jerusalem.

We stopped at the far end of the field for my husband to use the restroom. A man and boy were there. They had a nice light black skin, straight black hair and fine facial features. They wore regular clothing. The boy said he was 8 years old. He opened a door for my husband. He used an awl to open the door.

Interpreted by Athena 1/11/2008: These trees were olive and bearing bad fruit. The ground was similar to Yellowstone Geysers but not to that magnitude. This ground had underground caverns where gases escape. The boy opening the door means an unusual way of opening the door for your husband. You are to look up the number 8 in numerology and this is concerning your husband.

You were in the territory at the time Jesus was in that area, not Jerusalem, but the area he traveled to when he escaped after not being crucified. Although people think he was crucified, he was not killed.

The boy was the son of Jesus. Jesus had two girls and a boy—at the time you were traveling in but he had more children later. You were being given a tour—as you were making this journey, even though it was in your dream—you went through a part of Jerusalem. You saw the olive trees and the geysers. Then, when you traveled a little bit farther, it was to the grounds onto which Jesus escaped later, after his journey. The area today is known as Iraq. That is the dark skin and all, but for a brief time, Jesus and his son were present for you in that time period. You traveled back in time, an astral journey of the soul. You and your husband now are being allowed to astral travel and see this.

Athena: Your husband went to the restroom. You chose not to go because you knew you were in the presence of the Master and you chose to stay in his presence. Then that was the end of that journey. Now continue with the rest.

Just before waking for the day, I dreamed that my husband and I had a travel trailer. It was white. For some reason, we were driving to the old farmhouse where I was raised. I said we never had severe storms there so it should be safe. I considered my old home of my grandfather but recalled that none of our family lived there anymore.

Athena: Your were trying to select a safe area to be in when earth changes occur. The trailer being white means serenity, purity. You do not have to worry you are safe where you are. In your dream, your felt there would be more safety at your old home place. That is because there were times when you were growing up that you felt very safe where you lived.

On 1/6/2007, I dreamed that it was night and I was sitting in a chair on what seemed to be either a sunroom or a porch. The walls were white and about 4 feet tall. Then area had screens and possibly some type of windows. I heard a knock on the door in another area. I noticed a small pile of dirt on the floor near my chair and thought, overturned flowerpot. I was alert to the fact this was night time and unusual. I went to another room, Vicki ran in and fell on the floor obviously upset and scared. She seemed about 8 years old. I think someone was asleep in the room also. I went to pick her up and I woke up.

Later, Vicki e-mailed that she had been ill over the weekend with gastroenteritis. She was concerned because she also had pain in an old surgical site.

Interpretation on 1/11/2008 by Athena: The energy you were picking up in the dream state was that of Vicki being ill. The dirt on the floor was symbolic of the contamination of her body at that time. The knock on the door or the alarm was your soul being awakened to the fact she was experiencing discomfort.

The time has come to close for this session. Dr. Freud will be here the next time you come. He wants to talk with you more about the dreams and cell memory.

On 1/9/2007, I was walking with a man on a beach. He seemed okay. I saw tropical vegetation. At another point we were on a boat. There were several people on the boat. I observed what appeared to be a man in chains. He was treated badly by the man in charge and this man seemed to be the same one I had seen on the beach.

At another point, a group of women and I sat on a bed in a cabin. Soldiers came in to inspect the area. They did not bother us.

Interpretation by Athena 1/11/2008: This is a splinter soul of yours in a future life being lived now. It is a planet you've never heard of called Orclar. It is similar to Sicily, Italy in climate. You are living there now in the future; also, you are living a past life now. You proceeded to get off the boat. You also traveled by a new way of traveling. You were well paid and your type of work was undercover. The soldiers were in camouflage attire. Symbolically, their uniforms tell you the truth is disguised or hidden. The owner of the yacht was not an honest man.

1/10/2007. I had a very involved and disturbing dream. I will summarize the dream. I was in a room with my husband. I observed a silver colored calendar on the wall with a date marked and the name of a female. I realized it was the name of someone we had known. She was sick on and off for years before she died.

At some point, I felt that I was out of body observing my behavior. I threw a cup of water at the calendar or the wall and it went on the wall and floor. I thought this must be cleaned up. I didn't approve of my behavior.

Interpreted by Athena 1/11/2007: This dream was to give me opportunity to explain something to you. People carry or respond to stress in different ways. You tend to have fluid retention. The throwing of fluid on the wall was symbolic of your getting rid of your remaining stress and fluid retention.

The silver calendar on the wall was to tell you this represents the date the woman learned of her disease. The orbs on the calendar represent the people around her. Her last name in the dream was Hall. The individual has a record in the Hall of Records of the souls around her. Everyone, every human has such a record. You have one. Naomi has one.

The time has come to close for this session. Dr. Freud will be here the next time you come. He wants to talk with you more about the dreams and cell memory.

On 1/18/2008, Naomi said: We have guests escorted by Elijah. Elijah says: You have wonderful people helping you with the cell memory book. I will not tarry. Along with Dr. Freud is Sir Isaac Newton. Sir Newton is only here for a brief comment. He is not a loud mouth like me. Dr. Freud is coming to speak.

Dr. Freud

Dr. Freud: First of all, I want to thank you for your thoroughness on your dreams. Never, in all my work with people on earth or otherwise, have I seen anyone as dedicated as you are. You did exactly as I wanted you to do. I am delighted to tell you that you became aware that—as you had a dream and recorded it—the dreams increased. This showed your spiritual growth and the ability to dream, retain and bring the dream record to the one channeling for interpretation. You did a wonderful job with that.

Now, in composing the dreams that you have brought forth, I want you to stop. You may record the dreams but stop bringing them for interpretation. In the process of bringing them you have learned to interpret your own dreams. That was a training session for you and you accomplished it. Now, my dear, we are not saying that you have the ability to interpret everyone's dreams. You have the ability to interpret your dreams. Do not go out on a tangent and interpret dreams of others. Don't decide you want to be a professional dream interpreter. You have too much to do.

Dr. Freud: This work is very important to all souls that will survive. Because, after the earth has completed the earth changes, there will be the necessity to use the body parts of other people and so we need this information out so that those receiving the parts will not be alarmed about what is happening to them. There needs to be a guideline, an informative book of knowledge for them to have because the medical field is too scientific. They do not see that which I am giving to the one writing the book.

Sir Isaac Newton is with me listening and he was to participate in any discussion we have. He, even on this side, is one of few words. Sir Isaac is a contributing factor to your book. You may ask or think, why Sir Isaac Newton who worked in the *scientific field of gravitational pull*, and the *proving of the scientific method*. However, when on earth, he had another side.

He believed in what we are doing. He believed that after this life on earth that there was more. He was very dedicated to proving this and did not have the opportunity. So this is his opportunity and to help you bring forth evidence, very contrary to the medical community. Today, he is declining to speak. He does desire to be in on the beginning of the book, at this point. He wishes to help and assist. So, with his expertise in certain fields, we will be grateful for his help. Do you have questions?

Did you give me the five dreams last night? In one dream, there was a small man who showed me a barking dog. He said the dog's name was Hook. Was he Dr. Livingstone?

Dr. Freud: My dear, he is one who is working with us on the books. He had a life as Dr. Livingstone but he has been on earth more than once, as we all have. In your dream stage, he was with you. The five dreams complete all that you will bring here. Please stop at this point. After these five, you will not bring dreams for interpretation unless we request it. In the future, we will give some dreams and request that you bring them for more detailed explanations.

Our mission of your testing to see if you could recall and assess your dreams is complete. You came through like a trooper. That part of the mission is complete. You scored one hundred percent. We are proud of you. Bring any dreams not interpreted and we will work on those. End

6

Elijah: Opportunities

Elijah: There is a Council that reviews and approves souls to come to Earth. The purpose of coming to Earth is the *opportunity* to grow faster spiritually. This has been explained repeatedly.

There are a few things I want to review. They are the judgment and condemnation of others. Some people judge and condemn others of a different race, a different sexual orientation or different religions, or for other things. All of these people you meet are opportunities to choose. You may choose to like people who are different from yourself.

"On abortions, let me say: There is scientific evidence that says there is a human body in the womb—there is human tissue—but the soul of the unborn child did not enter the body. To Creator, the person is incomplete until the soul arrives. Sometimes the human person wishes to experience a stillborn. Sometimes the soul does not wish to go into the form at all and does not complete the life that could have been. This is to allow the parent to have the *opportunity* to seek from Creator that which it needs.

We use the word *opportunity* in all situations. Creator allows the experience. Allowing the experience opens the door for higher spiritual growth. Creator wanted me to go back over these points. This is not condemnation but an explanation as to why there are abortions, homosexuality, stillborns, alcoholics, and addicted people—to give opportunities. It gives opportunities to reach out and take their hands—not to put a knife in it—but to assist. Creator loves all, even the dark. Creator created light, those souls chose to go into the dark. That is not happiness for the Creator but he gives them opportunities to return to the light. If they do return to the light, he forgives, and they are one just as you are."

7

Dr. Carl Jung: Homosexuality

Dr. C. George Boeree wrote "Personality Theories," a lengthy article about the life of Carl Jung. The following information about Dr. Carl Jung was taken from that article. Carl Jung was born July 26, 1875 to parents that lived in the small Swiss village of Kessewil. His father was a country parson. Jung was surrounded by an extended family that included eccentrics and clergymen. (http://webspace.ship.edu/cgboer/jung.html)

As an adolescent, Jung didn't care for school. He attended boarding school and experienced jealous harassment. He then developed a tendency to faint under pressure. In later years, when it was time to choose a career, he first chose the field of archeology, then he switched to medicine and studied neurology awhile before switching to psychiatry. After graduation he worked in a mental hospital in Zurich under Eugene Bleuler, an expert in schizophrenia. He married in 1903 and also taught classes at the University of Zurich, had a private practice, and invented word association. Ibid.

Carl Jung admired the work of Sigmund Freud. They finally met in 1907 and talked for many hours. Jung worked with Freud and his group for a period of time. Since Jung was a younger man and very intelligent, Freud thought that Jung would continue the work he, Freud, had begun. It didn't happen. Although Jung was influenced by the work he did with Freud, he left that work group. Ibid.

Ultimately, Jung became well known for his own contributions to the field of psychiatry. He felt that "Anyone who wants to know the human psyche will learn next to nothing from experimental psychology. He would be better advised to abandon exact science, put away his scholar's gown, bid farewell to his study, and wander with human heart through the world. There in the horrors of prisons, lunatic asylums and hospitals, in drab suburban pubs, in brothels and gambling-hells, in the salons of the elegant, the Stock Exchanges, socialist meeting, churches, revivalist gatherings, and ecstatic sects, through love an hate, through the experience of passion in every form in his own body, he would reap richer stores of knowledge than text-books a foot thick could give him, and he will know how to doctor the sick with a real knowledge of the human soul." Carl Jung. Ibid.

Jung was known to have very lucid dreams on various topics and he was knowledgeable of dream symbols and the symbolism in mythology, religion and philosophy. He recorded his dreams and did paintings and sculptures based on his dreams. Ibid.

In his theories of the psyche, "Jung divides the psych into three parts. The first is the *ego,* which Jung identifies with the conscious mind. Closely related is the *personal unconscious,* which includes anything not presently conscious but could be. The personal unconscious is like most people's understanding of the unconscious in that it includes both memories that are easily brought to mind and those that have been suppressed for some reason. But it does not include the instincts that Freud would have it include." Ibid.

"Jung added part of the psyche that made his theory stand out from others, the *collective unconscious."* The *collective unconscious* is the reservoir of our experiences as a species, a kind of knowledge we are all born with. And yet we can never be directly conscious of it. It influences all of our experiences and behaviors, especially the emotional ones . . ."

The article also goes on to state that some experiences show the effect of the collective unconscious more clearly than others. An example given was the near death experiences. People of various cultures, beliefs, and nationalities, have given accounts of what they saw, felt, and recognized. They all have similar recollections when brought back from death.

Jung developed extensive assessment tools for defining and describing various personality types. A few words associated with his work in this area include introvert, extrovert, transcendence, entropy, and synchronicity. Jung, when compared to Freud, was described as more of an "anything goes" type. Freud was more formal and rigid. Jung died in 1961. Ibid.

Carl Jung channeled the following material from the Beyond:

Naomi: A high spiritual energy stated that Creator wants this line in the cell memory book. "The cell memory carries the attributes to be of sexual male or female or what is labeled gay."

Dr. Jung: "What a pleasure to appear on Earth again in a form different from human. This work you are doing is quite intriguing. On this side we are quite exposed to many facets of paranormal, as you call it on Earth. When I was on Earth, I had my theories in my work. Some were correct and some were not, as I found out after I crossed over. I did not come today to expand on my abilities or my faults.

First, you know that Earth is considered a school of learning. Earth is a planet within a planetary system, which happens to be less important. Earth and the planetary system it occupies is one of the lesser planetary systems. It is less recognized and less important to most in other planetary systems and universes. In other words, when I say less of a planet, or less than other planetary systems, that is the summation of all other planetary dignitaries. To Creator all are equal.

Now, in the information I am to give, I am going to stick with humans on Earth because that is what you and the people that read your books are familiar with. Therefore, I will get right to the point of homosexuality and how it is related to cell memory.

Homosexuality and how it is related to the cell memory is a simple one. The Creator—upon creating the cells themselves—placed within the cells, not only the DNA—but everything associated with DNA—and anything that would relate to DNA in any planetary system or any universe anywhere. The DNA and the other consistencies within the cell itself allow this for balance. The DNA is a structure and it will remain so.

Once the DNA occupies any form—the making of the human form or any other form used in any other planetary system—once this occurs, the cell structure being combined and made in all existence is by Creator. Creator knew that cells needed balance. Humans need balance. Within the cell structure is allotted so many materials—I could give a name—I will give you an example, you know of chromosomes—this is not chromosomes. This is an identity given to this structure—to make it simple—for those that read your book—is the material for female/male which goes back to the chromosomes. That is in the physical.

Now the balancing—that which is not physical—is the sexual aspect of masculinity and femininity. The Creator has a balancing mechanism within the DNA for femininity and masculinity. Therefore, the free will enters the picture of all who exist and come into a form that contains DNA.

Free will—meaning that on this side—in constructing their charts, they have the free will to be on any planetary system, as a masculine or as a feminine form. The structure, being as it is, and Creator requesting balance—some upon dwelling in the human forms, or in other forms on other planetary systems, prefer one system over the other. In other words, some may prefer the masculine form in which they would hunt or go to war or whatever traits or characteristics the masculine of that area would have. For the purpose of balance, suppose the soul had ten lives to live on Earth, five of these should be lived as male and five as female.

Now, this is only my theory—Carl Jung's theory—of how homosexuality occurs. These souls, upon electing to come to any planetary system as a masculine or feminine form get carried away with what they prefer. They indeed have free will. They may indeed have ten lifetimes that should have been five feminine and five masculine.

Instead, suppose the soul chose five lives of the masculine and then they took on the masculine the next three times. That is eight times straight as masculine. This then, is when you would have the homosexuality, the imbalance. You would have the three lives lived as male, which, for balance, should have been lived as female. The male in this situation lives in the human male form but has the female traits and characteristics because it must balance.

The converse would be true for the soul that preferred the female form and chose five lives straight as female and then chose another three as female. For balance, the soul would live three lives in a female form but have male traits and characteristics.

You would have to be here to really understand this. Creator—in a Creator type way—issues a request that goes to Jamiah, Oshinbah, and so on down the line, until we reach the soul level of the individual that prefers to do this. The soul is informed that it has used up the free choices it had to balance. Now, there are no more free choices balance must occur. This is how homosexuality occurs.

Only on Earth is sexual activity censured and taken apart in a negative way. Earth is a school and the sexual urge on Earth is to reproduce so that more humans may come onto Earth to learn the lessons they come to learn. This is the only planet that is provided sexual abilities that stick strictly to the feminine or masculine.

In other words, on other planetary systems, wherever the souls may locate, there may be no sex, no urge for sex, or no desire for sex. The reproductive action is done in a manner that is different from that of Earth. All planets and planetary systems have their own methods and mannerisms. I won't go into detail because they are too varied and it would take centuries to tell you all the different methods.

To keep it simple, planet Earth is your school. Planet Earth is where you go to reproduce to give more souls the opportunity to learn. The reproduction process is similar in all species on Earth. For example, if you study the reptile and insect worlds, you will note that they reproduce by different methods. The point is, I came today to say to you: Homosexuality is developed after each soul decides. If this soul decides to not balance when it comes on Earth, then it will be balanced by the process of the system of going from Creator, to Jamiah, to Oshinbah and on down—let's call it ranks.

Homosexuality is simple. Although on this side that I am now on, we see no problem with any of it. It is just a means of bringing opportunities to Earth so that others may experience that which they came to learn. That is all the sexual should be.

Getting back to the core of the matter, homosexuality is when the soul has entered into a human body and is trying to balance the feminine and masculine. I have already stated how this occurs. Each soul experiencing this balancing process has desires and beliefs so strong that they live out their lives trying to balance the masculine and feminine. Until recent years, society rejected all of this. Homosexuals were persecuted, tortured, and even killed because of their sexual preference.

Now, let me inform you, getting back to where I am now in other planetary systems, in the field of scientific research, it matters not to us or Creator how you perform the sexual act. I am getting off this subject a little bit but it is still related to it. The sexual act on any planetary system in any universe is just a means of staying in touch with Creator.

Sexual release, what you call orgasm, is the same experience you have on this side when souls blend together. Only on Earth is there a problem of multiple partners. We do not encourage this; do not misunderstand. But the act of orgasms on Earth is a reuniting of souls. We on this side and in other planetary systems simply blend the souls together and have the same feeling that you would have upon an orgasm on Earth.

How you arrive at an orgasm on Earth—if you are homosexual and you use devices or your own pleasured way, it is nothing to Creator. There is no objection from Creator or others on this side that are very much informed, as you will be when you return. They are very much informed and know that there is nothing negative, dirty, or unhealthy about having emotions that involve orgasms. The soul from Creator on this side still has the emotional. It has a form and none will believe this on Earth. But this needs to be in this book.

By Creator's instruction: Orgasms of any form, however they may be derived are nothing but pure love—love from Creator. Orgasms are nothing of a dirty nature. They are nothing of the obscene nature. Orgasms are love. Orgasms are a form of becoming one with Creator again. That was given to all, no matter where you exist or in what form you exist, Creator comes through. Over here we do not call it orgasms—we just do love. There may be groups of ten souls in one group and fifteen souls in another group and you blend together. It is like ectoplasm or two bowls of different colors of Jello blending together. Humans have just made this blending together something obscene and this is incorrect. It is a closeness with God and becoming one with God.

I hope that I have not steered too far from the path of describing what homosexuality is. I was instructed by Creator to come and give you the scientific reason and the purpose for having to be masculine/feminine. If you have questions you may ask them now.

I, Grace, replied that I understand that there is no moral issue or judgment here. However, here on Earth we have diseases such as AIDS (acquired autoimmune deficiency syndrome) and STDs (sexually transmitted diseases). Some of these are said to result from risky sexual behavior, such as multiple partners and unprotected sex. As a result, fears, judgments, labels and various emotional responses occur. In health care, this has been a major concern in infection control and cost of care. What can be done?

Dr. Jung replied: "Maybe I can explain why there is "dis-ease." These humans that you refer to, as multiple partners that end up with "dis-ease," expect disease. This is because, in earths' terms, they have done something incorrect. You will note that your animals on Earth do not have diseases because they have multiple partners. The reason is that they do not have a conscience. They have a sexual urge, a physical urge. For example, the dogs—there will be six or eight male dogs trying to pleasure the female dog. No disease results from that.

Now, I believe, they have applied blame to the monkeys in Africa for transmitting the disease of Aids. This is not a disease among the monkeys. They do not die from this. This is something humans acquired by copying the monkeys because humans have a higher intellect, supposedly, that says it is not right to do this.

Creator would prefer that humans remain loyal to each other (one-to-one). Because once they come back over here, once you hurt someone, then you have to answer for that. This is the only reason that

Creator would prefer this. Creator would prefer this and this is how it was in the early days of the Cave Man era and human life. There was no guilt because they did not know what guilt was. When jealousy/emotions began arriving in the human body was when problems began." End

8

Jamiah: Abortions

"Creator say to Jamiah, explain to you in Earth terms and you write. Tell of cell memory. Tell all have DNA. DNA and cell memory stored in each human and it awakes at the time needed.

Now, Rainbow Children coming on Earth. They have other strand of DNA. Tests not accurate. When mommy carry baby and get test, test not show accurate. The medical wish to abort—no, no, no—do not abort. These are Rainbow Children. Mommies do not need test. Creator say—Mommies do not abort. You see, many more Rainbow Children coming now. Creator say: Mommies must not abort Rainbow Children coming. Get book out so enlighten, stop destruction of soul's dwelling. Whew! This above Jamiah's head."

I asked: Is there a way to identify the DNA of a Rainbow baby as opposed to a truly abnormal fetus, for example a Downs Syndrome baby or one with severe genetic problems? Jamiah answered: "No need to. See, one you call Down's syndrome or other, contract exists with that soul and parent. If done away with, not serve purpose. Meant to be."

I asked does that mean that there should not be any abortions? Jamiah said: "No, that not correct. Many abortions okay because soul not ready to come, mommy not ready. Better to take mass out of body—not human, not breathing, not developed—it like a growth. No sin, no problem to do away with what they cannot handle or soul here not ready to come. Jamiah have hard time explaining."

I said everyone on Earth has problems with the issue of abortion. There are many battles over this and whether it is right or wrong, good or bad. Jamiah again stated that abortion is good for those that want it, for example, when the mother is not ready or the soul is not ready come. The mothers do not need the DNA tests. The Rainbow Children are normal.

9

Edgar Cayce: Abortions

I want to inform you that—once the soul is created—the DNA and cell memory stay with the soul throughout. That means that you may be on another planet or in another planetary system even, but your DNA and cell memory remain with you wherever you are or have been. You carry it forward each time. You cannot destroy the system of DNA.

In the newborns, if any of you have children under age 20, those are either the Rainbow Children (more of them are under age 14) or they are the Indigo Children. These, of that age group, do not have the normal DNA strand. Therefore, when tests are done, especially when the mother is carrying the child, there will be an abnormality in most tests administered during pregnancy. The test will show the child to have an abnormal condition. And many women choose to abort at that time. That is not a wise choice. These souls have extra strands of DNA. Now, if you know anyone in that age group, or any childbearing female or parent, inform the individual—even if they do not believe what you are stating—they need to be informed. It will enter their thought processes enough that perhaps they would not abort a fetus.

Edgar wishes to inform you that we on this side do not condemn abortions. The reason is the life force, the soul, each soul chooses to enter at the time it desires. Remember this if you remember nothing else. We have access to the charts. That soul that is to enter the Earth makes a choice as to when to enter or not enter the female body that carries the fetus. Some choose to never enter; they do not want the confinement. They wait until the birth—the expelling of the child—is complete. Others choose to experience and they enter at five to five and a half months. Before that timeframe, as our records show, no soul enters the fetus state the first five months.

We do not condone abortions for reasons of emotions, disgrace or convenience. It is important in the emotional but what we know on this

130

side is that there is no spirit or soul in these formations. So, to throw guilt upon a young mother or young lady because she chooses abortion before five months, we would appreciate society not doing that. It is a choice. Also, on the other end of the spectrum, do not abort at all because DNA shows (the fetus has) a physical problem. DNA tests themselves are not accurate, as far as the test administered. The DNA is accurate. The tests may be administered wrongly or without proper training. My point is do not pass judgment on anyone for any condition they have or for ceasing of a condition, which brings the opposite into viewpoint which is suicide.

10

Edgar Cayce: Suicide

"Edgar does not know that if you have family or know of anyone who ended his or her life by self-destruction. There are many who want to come onto Earth to speed up the process of spiritual growth.

Then, when they come on Earth, they cannot handle the different human aspects. They cannot handle the emotional aspects or the physical aspects. This is so for their whole body system. They choose to leave. That is what you call suicide. That soul did not harm itself, except—now listen carefully—except the soul came on Earth to learn a lesson—to make progress by learning. It left without doing this. So, it still must experience this. However, the next time the soul comes to the planet of learning—be it Earth or Venus—the next time before it comes, it will be taking into itself consideration as to where and what, instead of rashly entering without proper training.

We do have on this side a Council that conducts a thorough interview with these souls and advises them to not come, or if they do come, to prepare in a certain way. Even if they do prepare and come, the experience may be too much for them to endure. Do not pass judgment on that or the abortion process.

Our Creator forgives. Creator forgives. Creator loves. There is never a punishment. These souls have to debrief, work through and reprogram. To debrief, they enter a building where many souls surround them and project love into the soul that left the physical human form by suicide.

Much guilt is projected onto others when society learns of a suicide or abortion. That's why Edgar took this opportunity to explain the consequences.

There is a verse. It is in the Bible but it applies without it being in the Bible: Judge not lest ye be judged also. Do not judge others. It only slows your soul growth. When you take on the position of our Creator and declare a judgment on anyone, you have slowed your progress in the growth of spirit. This was a request from Creator that I address this."

11

Organ Transplants and Cell Memories

As I pondered how to proceed to the subject of organ transplants—a topic about which I knew little—I had an unexpected guest in a dream one morning. In the dream, a former boss—one that I respected and liked—came and held out his hand. He dropped into my left hand gold earrings with white pearls. I was excited to see him. I knew he was Mr. G. He spoke to me by thought about others we knew. He said enough that we both knew we were on the same page.

He started talking in the dream and, as I awoke, he continued to speak by thought. I went to my kitchen table—where I keep a pad and pen—I sat down and wrote what he said, as he spoke. He told me not to worry if I missed a word because he or someone else would return for any corrections. The whole experience felt natural—like I had visited with Mr. G. His thoughts were completely clear to me in content and word selection. Even in thought, the words "sounded" as he would have spoken them.

I then dressed and went to my session with Naomi. Mr. G. met me there and channeled through her to me. When he appeared to Naomi, he told her that at work I had called him an initial. This was true and for this book, I changed the initial. Also, Elijah was with Mr. G., at Naomi's, teaching him how to channel through her. The following is a portion of the information channeled directly to me.

Mr. G.

Cell memory is the transmission of recorded personality characteristics and traits—thoughts, feelings, emotions, habits or programs—from one living cell to another. Or stated another way, the transmission of recorded characteristics and traits from the cells of one organ in a human body to another organ in a human body. The cells of a transplanted organ are containers for the characteristics and traits of the physical form in which they developed.

On Earth this cell is in human form, a living organism of flesh, tissue. This tissue requires sufficient oxygenation by good lungs and blood circulation, a good heart that keeps blood circulating to the brain and to the tissues throughout the body. Without proper circulation to all the tissues of the body, the body ceases to function. The excretory systems of the human body must function effectively to rid the body of toxins. The various organs and systems of the body must operate as an integrated balanced machine. In many ways it is comparable to a computer. In that sense, the brain would be the operating system that enables functions. The soul would be the master motherboard that knows all and hears all and records all for each soul. Each soul has done so since that soul was created and chose, along with Creator, its eternal purpose. The soul responds to all based upon the chart made prior to each birth and choices made by the human after the soul enters the human form.

This goes back to the information given by Jamiah, Oshinbah, Celonious, Elijah, and others on cell memory. How human bodies on earth were designed and grew in size and intellect and had access to Creator Himself/Herself. In the beginning, this was a very much like the Garden of Eden. There was peace, love, and people knew what they could eat, drink, and do. This lasted until the dark energy of evil—jealousy, envy and such—entered the earth. Over time, the evil presented a challenge to the souls of the good, the souls of the White Light. It has been and remains a struggle between good and evil.

Souls that stay connected to the Creator of all that is and to God over our Earth grow spiritually. Many different prophets have been sent to Earth to teach man to live in love, peace, harmony and caring for each other. Even these teachings were distorted by the dark energies and became fear, intimidation, jealousy and hatred. Choices made and actions taken produced diseases, plagues, wars, and such. Earth has now reached the point of no return. It must be cleansed of the dark, the fear, the greed, and the negativity and diseases that result. The time of an Earth changing cataclysm is fast approaching. There will be much chaos and much restructuring in all we have learned to a take for granted. What does all this have to do with cell memory?

Recall all that has been given about DNA and cell memory. When Creator made souls, each was made with a cell of the Creator and therefore, each cell has an exact copy of the DNA and cell memory of the Creator. That is how we are all connected. That's how He/She keeps track of us—hears our cries for help and expressions of gratitude for blessings, hears our thanks for liberty and freedom to choose, and hears our thanks for our health, our children and our opportunities to grow spiritually. In other words our soul growth here on Earth depends upon the choices we make in our daily lives. As has been said often by Elijah, "it is not what you go through but how you go through it."

If we allow negative emotions such as fear, anger, resentment, prejudice, hatred, jealousy to rule, these create cell memory problems. If we cause another to have emotional or physical pain from actions such as betrayal of a spouse, excessive control, emotional abuse, physical abuse and such, then that creates negative cell memories which must be cleared and forgiven by parties involved. All parties involved must clear and forgive in order to grow spiritually. Each is accountable for his or her clearing. There is however another scenario, if an individual forgives himself and the other person and tries to make peace, but the other person or persons refuse peace/forgiveness, then it is they who have and are stuck with the problem. Cell memories of emotional pain and trauma, if not cleared, are carried from life to life and do cause problems.

Now, as stated previously, cells have memory. Cells make up organs and tissues of the human body. Now we approach the subject of *organ transplants*. We will try to keep this simple. The organs of heart, lung, kidney, liver, and pancreas are transplanted. The process of preparing a person emotionally and physically to receive a transplanted organ is a delicate and tedious matter. On the emotional level, the patient and family in this situation are already experiencing the stages of grief. These are denial, anger, bargaining, depression and acceptance. At the same time, they are hoping for a miracle—a cure or a donor organ/organs that match the needs of the patient. Also, another conflict is the emotion of knowing that another person will lose his/her life in order for this other patient or family member to live.

Mr. G. made several other comments and then said that he works with physicians on the Other Side. The doctors do research. He provides the doctors with supplies they request. His purpose in the visit to me was to see if I could receive what he said directly to me, without Naomi. I did receive Mr. G. accurately alone. Now, Mr. G. can return with information when others are busy. This was just a test. End

Now, for me personally, the situation of a parent donating a child's organs is one I find hard to even imagine. As a society we believe that children outlive the parents. Caring for a very ill child or the body of dead child was among the most difficult things I have ever done. I specifically recall such a case. I was a student nurse in a Pediatric Unit taking care of a little boy about age four. He was scheduled for heart surgery the next morning early and was supposed to be back in his crib by midnight of my next shift. When I went on duty, his crib was empty and his name was gone. He had died in surgery. I was age twenty and felt horrible for days. I knew then that I could never work in pediatrics.

Today, Naomi and I know a lady who donated her son's organs in 1989 and she is still struggling with his loss. Several people were recipients of his organs but she only heard from one. She still has not had closure. She has not dreamed of her son and finds it very painful to speak of him. And still, in her mind, she wonders if some part of him is still alive after all these years. The lady is an elderly waitress/cashier who now has trouble walking. Even though Naomi often eats at the restaurant where the lady works and had seen her for years in the restaurant, it was only recently that Naomi learned the lady had lost a son. One day, the lady just started talking about this to Naomi.

So now, Naomi and I are trying to assist her. I gave her a set of my books and she said she reads a few pages every night. She said the material is helping her emotionally and that she had not read anything like this before. She would like to hear from anyone who received an organ from her son. With our assistance and encouragement, she is now working through the local donor services unit to acquire responses from recipients of her son's organs.

The following are organ transplant cases that I selected to present. All, except one of these organ recipients spoke of receiving cell memories of the donor.

Case 1

Sierra Sekulich

"A mother's gift Her 'babies' died; their organs let 9 live" was the title of a front-page article of *The Tennessean*, on Sunday, July 16, 2006. I have read numerous cases of organ transplants, but this one was among the most brutally honest and informative. The story—by Mitchell Kline, Staff Writer—filled two inside pages. With consent of the newspaper, I chose excerpts from this special story of lives lost and lives saved by organ transplants—as told by exceptional people involved in the cases.

Kimberly Rushing McCulley experienced the tragedy of losing two children in less than a year. "Her daughter, Desiree, was struck and killed by a car on November 15, 2004. Less than a year later, her sixteen-year-old son, Nicholas Rushing, was shot and killed by a friend."

"McCulley, age thirty-seven, allowed doctors to take vital organs from both of her children so that someone, somewhere could have a second chance. Nine lives were saved as a result." Only one of the cases, Sierra Sekulich, was discussed at length.

Sierra was the first person to have a heart and double-lung transplant performed by doctors at the Monroe Carell Jr. Children's Hospital at Vanderbilt in Nashville, Tennessee. Sierra, at age fifteen, was suffering from a genetic disease and this surgery saved her life.

When Sierra was a newborn baby doctors discovered that she had a heart murmur and she had surgery for this at eight months of age. "Then 9 years later, an aneurysm developed on the patch covering the hole. She was rushed to surgery and later given medication that her doctors thought would allow her to live a relatively normal life. But optimism had faded by May 2005, when Sierra's lung pressure began a dangerous and steady climb."

Sierra described her breathing as feeling like she was "breathing through a coffee straw." By October, Sierra was "too weak to go the bathroom. She routinely passed out while sitting up. Doctors told her mother she wouldn't make it to Thanksgiving without a transplant, but three possible donors were passed over in the hope of finding a more suitable match."

Sierra's mother, Anna Sekulich said that she had to have a serious talk with Sierra about "whether to go on life support to buy more time." Also, she informed her daughter that "if this had become too much and she wanted to stop the fight, that she would not be mad."

Sierra and Anna planned Sierra's funeral, as hope for a matched heart and two lungs faded. Then in November Sierra dreamed that she received the needed organs. And later, on November 8, 2005 about 11:00 a.m., they received the call.

Unknown at the time, the donor of needed organs would be Nicholas Rushing, age sixteen, who was shot in the head by a friend. He was rushed to Vanderbilt Hospital where he later died and his mother donated his organs. Later that day at Vanderbilt Hospital, Sierra Sekulich received the heart and lungs of Nicholas Rushing. Dr. Frank Scholl, a cardio thoracic surgeon, led the surgical team that performed the twelve-hour surgery.

Nicholas Rushing, the son of Kimberly (Rushing) McCulley had known grief and pain in the past. Nick's father and his mother, Kimberly, divorced when he was a toddler and Nick went to live with his dad. Later his father married Nina Rushing. In April 2003, the father of Nicholas died and Nicholas continued to live with his stepmother, Nina. According to Kimberly, Nicholas had a difficult time accepting the death of his father. Then the following year his sister died crossing a highway in Dickson, Tennessee. On the night of her death, Desiree had just come off being grounded and was allowed to go to the movies with friends. She was dropped off at the movie theater. Some of the friends ran across the street to an arcade, but Desiree did not make it across.

Several months after losing Nicholas, through a series of unusual events, Kimberly was able to meet the girl who received the heart and both lungs of her son. Her name was Sierra Sekulich. She also met Sierra's mother Anna. Upon the first meeting of the mothers, questions arose. Anna Sekulich wanted to know what kind of person Nick was. His mom described him as loving, caring, compassionate and a people person.

Anna then asked about foods he liked and his habits. Did he like eggs and did he keep his room clean? She asked because—before surgery—Sierra refused eggs completely. Also, she was lactose intolerant. "She could not eat chocolate or ice cream or milk and you couldn't pay the child to eat eggs. Now she begs for scrambled eggs. She doesn't have a problem drinking milk."

Kimberly McCulley confirmed that her son Nick "had a taste for eggs and liked milk products.

Anna Sekulich said that her daughter Sierra "began to exhibit different personality traits following the transplant. She now prefers a clean room, listens to rap music and likes camouflage—all things Nicholas preferred."

Sierra herself refers to "Nick days" and "Sierra days." A Nick days means eggs, bacon and straightening up to the tune of "Baby Got Back". A Sierra day means doughnuts, the color pink, wisecracks and clothes on the floor.

McCulley saw some of Desiree's traits in Sierra as well. She was feisty, had a strong sense of who she was, and stood up for what she believed was right. In her mind, McCulley felt that her children had passed along more than their vital organs.

These two mothers have become friends. Kimberly likes to feel Nick's heart beat in Sierra's chest. Sierra and Anna Sekulich are grateful for the new life Nick's heart and lungs provided. The article emphasizes the emotions that both families experience during this ordeal. While the Sekulich family is happy over successful organ transplant surgery, there is also sadness that another family lost a child that made this possible. That family is the Kimberly McCulley family. The death of Nicholas means this family has lost two children within a year. But, Kimberly's decision to donate Nick's organs helped others survive. And, feeling Nick's heart beat in the chest of Sierra helped Kimberly feel a part of him that continues to live. (Mitchell Klein 2006)

Case 2

The late Dr. Paul Pearsall documented numerous interviews with organ transplant recipients. Selected cases of heart transplants were presented in his book *The Heart's Code*. (Also, numerous cases were presented on his web site: PaulPearsall.com). He chose cases in which a family member was able to verify the patient's cell memory story. Cases below are examples of these.

Pearsall's first case in his book *The Heart's Code* was a forty-one-year-old male who received the heart of a nineteen-year-old girl killed when her car was struck by a train.

After the transplant, the patient stated, "I felt it when I woke up. You know how it feels different after a thunderstorm or heavy rain? You know that feeling in the air? That's kind of how it felt. It was like a storm had happened inside me or like I had been struck by lightning. There is a new energy in me. I feel like nineteen again. I'm sure I got a strong young man's heart because sometimes I can feel like a roar or surging power within me that I never felt before. I think he was probably a truck diver or something like that, and he was probably killed by a cement truck or something like that. I feel this sense of speed and raw power in me." (Paul Pearsall 1998)

The recipient's wife stated: "He's a kid again. He used to struggle to breathe and had no stamina at all, but now he's like a teenager. The transplant changed him completely. He keeps talking about power and energy all the time. He says he has had several dreams that he is driving a huge truck or is the engineer of a large steam engine. He is sure that his donor was driving a big truck that hit a bigger truck." Ibid

Case 3

Pearsall's third case was a thirty-five year old female heart transplant recipient. The donor was a twenty-four old prostitute killed in a stabbing.

The recipient's statements were: "I never really was all that interested in sex. I never really thought about it much. Don't get me wrong, my husband and I had a sex life, but it was not a big part of our life. Now, I tire my husband out. I want sex every night and I masturbate two to three times a day sometimes. I used to hate x-rated videos, but now I love them. I feel like a slut sometimes and I even do a strip for my husband when I'm in the mood. I would never have done that before my surgery. When I told my psychiatrist about this, she said it was a reaction to my medications and my healthier body. Then I found out that my donor was a young college girl that worked as a topless dancer and in an out-call service. I think I got her sexual drive, and my husband agrees. He says I'm not the woman he married, but he wants to marry me again."

The husband's reply: "Not that I'm complaining, mind you, but what I have now is a sex kitten. It's not that we do it more, but she wants to talk about sex more and wants to see sexually explicit tapes, which I could never talk her into before. When we do have sex, its different. Not worse or better, just different. She never talked much during sex, but now she practically narrates the whole thing. She uses words I never heard her use before, but it kind of turns me on so who's complaining? Our worst argument came a few months after her transplant and well before she knew who her donor was. I was joking and at a passionate moment said that she must have gotten the heart of a whore. We didn't talk for weeks." Ibid.

Case 4. Another case reported by Pearsall is one that I first read in a magazine years ago. Now it is a case often cited in books, magazines and on the Internet. The case is that of an eight-year-old girl who received the heart of a ten-year-old girl that had been murdered. Prior to the transplant the child did not have nightmares according to the mother. After the transplant the child had repeated nightmares. As it turned out, she was dreaming of the donor child's murder. Her descriptions were so vivid that the child's mother took the child to a psychiatrist. Recognizing the unusual graphic descriptions the child related, the psychiatrist and the mother notified the police. The child was able to describe the murder scene, what clothing the child and murderer wore and what they said to each other. With that evidence, police were able to arrest the murderer. Similar cases were also reported. (Leslie A. Takeuchi 2010)

The following paragraphs were taken from the same article by Leslie A. Takeuchi, which was posted on the Internet: "Although medical science is not ready to embrace the ideas of cellular memory, one surgeon believes there must be something to it. Mehmet Oz, MD, heart surgeon at Columbia Presbyterian Medical Center, has invited an energy healer, Julie Motz, into the operating room during transplant surgery. Initially, Motz practiced energy healing to help reduce anxiety prior to surgery and depression following surgery. Then the team noticed that there seemed to be less incidence of rejection in these patients. They were curious to see what would happen if she were present during the operation. Motz registers, through sensations in her own body, the emotional state of the patient during the surgical procedure. Through her touch or words, Motz attempts to alleviate any worries, fears or anger the patient may be experiencing. She works with the recipient's ability to accept the new organ and also works with the donated tissue so it will accept a new body. The results have been favorable and the team reports reduced rejection and increased survival rates. This may sound outrageous to those who never thought about tissues having feelings or caring about where they would reside, but Dr. Oz believes that it would be a disservice to ignore even the possibility that this method could help." Ibid.

Takeuchi said, "Intriguing questions remain. What percentage of transplant recipients actually do feel changes in behavior and personality or report changes in food preferences or have new memories? Is there a higher incidence of tissue or organ acceptance in those patients who are aware of their consciousness or who have energy work done? Will ordinary science offer more evidence to support that memories are transferred or will we need a new science? Perhaps more importantly, what does this transcendent phenomenon have to tell us about other healing events?" Ibid.

Case 5

"The donor was a 19-year-old woman killed in an automobile accident. The recipient was a 29-year old woman diagnosed with cardiomyopathy secondary to endocarditis." (Paul Pearsall et. al. 2005)

The donor's mother reported: My daughter Sara was the most loving girl. She owned and operated her own health food restaurant and scolded me constantly about not being a vegetarian. She was a great kid. Wild but great. She was into the free-love thing and had a different man in her life every few months. She was man crazy when she was a little girl and it never stopped. She was able to write some notes to me when she was dying. She was out of it, but she kept saying how she could feel the impact of the car hitting them. She said she could feel it going through her body." Ibid.

The recipient reported: You can tell people this if you want to, but it will make you sound crazy. When I got my new heart, two things happened to me. First, almost every night, and still sometimes now, I actually feel the accident my donor had. I can feel the impact in my chest. It slams into me, but my doctor said everything looks fine. Also, I hate meat now. I can't stand it. I was McDonald's biggest money-maker, and now meat makes me throw-up. Actually, when I smell it, my heart starts to race. But that's not the big deal. My doctor says it is just due to my medicines." Ibid.

"I couldn't tell him, but what really bothers me is that I'm engaged to be married now. He's a great guy and we love each other. The sex is terrific. The problem is, I'm gay. At least, I thought I was. After my transplant, I'm not . . . I don't think . . . anyway . . . I'm sort of semi-or confused gay. Women still seem attractive to me but my boyfriend turns me on; women don't. I have absolutely no desire to be with a woman. I think I got a gender transplant." Ibid.

The recipient's brother reported: "Susie is straight now. I mean it seriously. She was gay and now her new heart made her straight. She threw out all books and stuff about gay politics and never talks about it any more. She was really militant about it before. She holds hands and cuddles with Steven just like my girlfriend does with me. She talks girl talk with my girlfriend, where before she would be lecturing about the evils of sexist men. And my sister, the queen of the Big Mac, hates meat. She won't even have it in the house." Ibid

Case 6

Claire Sylvia had a heart-lung transplant in 1997 at Yale-New Haven Hospital. Thereafter, she and coauthor, William Novak, published her story, *A Change of Heart*. (I read her book years ago). Her story was probably the first story I read about a heart transplant. She reported that she records her dreams in a journal. She was not supposed to know the identity of her donor but she did because she dreamed his identity. She noticed changes In her attitude, food preferences, color preferences in clothing and behavior changes. She did not like Chicken Nuggets but he did. She became more aggressive like her male donor, an eighteen year old killed in a motorcycle accident. She was persistent and eventually met the family of the young man who was her donor and was able to learn what he was like as a person. Ibid.

Case 7

Amy Silverstein also had a heart transplant and published her ordeal in *Trial by Transplant*. I read the book excerpt in U. S. News and World Report. Amy's story is worth reading. She describes the pain of numerous heart biopsies—she "white knuckled her way through more than 60" and painful defibrillations sometimes followed biopsies. She described in great detail how it felt to have a doctor make numerous attempts to obtain a biopsy and how it felt to have pieces of a beating heart snipped for the study. After her transplant, she seemed to have traded one set of problems for another set. She tells in graphic detail how she felt about the new heart and what it was like to live with it. The heart never felt like her own and never functioned like her own. "It is not possible to reattach the bloody tangle of dangling nerve fibers." (Amy Silverstein 2007)

She described how her life revolved around doctor visits, taking immunosuppressive drugs and complications. The drugs killed her immune system and she developed tumors and the threat of cancer. She said her heart had a ten-year shelf life but she seems to have lived seventeen years with the transplanted heart. She had excellent doctors. She had excellent support of family and friends. She felt they all grew weary of her ongoing needs. I don't know whether in her book she became more positive or how her life ended. Ibid.

Numerous other transplant cases are posted on the Internet. Many speak of various changes after kidney transplants. Some speak not only of the changes of food, colors, and clothing preferences but changes in music, art, and literature preferences. Some even spoke of improved skills in music, writing and art. End

Part III

Use of DNA and Cell Memory

1

Overview: Soul Origin and Energy Levels

Dreams, meditation, and hypnosis are three methods to clear cell memory. This is information that has been given through Naomi—not only to me, but also other clients—by those who have channeled information from our Creator. Before we get into the specifics and examples of these, it is important to understand that in all we do we are working with energy. This energy is of the soul and we need to keep the energy as pure and balanced as possible by the choices we make. It *sounds simple. It is simple.* Our Creator sent messengers to give us accurate information in *simple words* so that all may understand and hopefully benefit.

This section contains information given in channeling and also review of literature that was placed in my path, as I approached this section. From some ten books I purchased and reviewed, three really stood out for this section. These will be shared later. But first an overview of information I was recently given about our Creator—the Source—the energy of all that is. This is the energy of our origin—the energy, which is inside of us and the energy, which is outside of us—is in all things. We interact with each other at all times. We are, in a sense, co-creators.

First, Creator is neither male nor female. Our Creator created the energies called masculine and feminine. Those that channel refer to Creator as He/She. When Creator made anything, including the human soul, He began with one cell. For this section, I am speaking of the *human soul cell that lives within the human physical form.* The human soul cell container has a nucleus, which contains DNA and cell memory and that was placed there by the Creator, the I Am, or the Source of All that exists. *This soul DNA is not traceable by humans on earth doing research.* I have repeatedly asked if it is possible to trace the *soul DNA* from one life to the next and I have been told no, the soul DNA is not traceable, as the physical DNA is traceable. Again, even in organ transplants, souls do not mix. Cell walls of the soul serve as barriers that seem to recognize what belongs and what does not belong to that soul. Only Creator has complete access to the soul or the complete records of the soul. Others designated or approved by Creator work with different aspects of the soul, but only Creator has full access, and only Creator knows all the aspects of a given soul.

The *soul DNA and cell memory* is how Creator recognizes each of us. He knows our location, and history, our thoughts and actions daily. He knows our needs and hears our requests. He knows our positive emotions and acts of love, compassion and empathy. These keep us connected to him and expand our soul growth. He also knows our emotions of fear, anger, rage, and hate. He knows feelings of frustration, depression and helplessness, as we struggle with the lessons learned through emotions. This same DNA and cell memory of our soul produce the permanent record with our Creator and in the Hall of Records. This is how and where all records of all souls of all universes are kept, maintained, and updated. Remember the word updated. Our soul record is updated, as our soul reincarnates and completes journeys we chart for the purpose of soul growth. As we live each day of a life anywhere, daily, the soul record is updated.

Other planetary systems have environments that are different from that of Earth. Therefore, the forms the soul, our souls, would inhabit there are different from us *in appearance. Understand that the form is different and the building blocks of that form are in response to that environment.* The form adapts to the environment in order to survive. The soul living in the form is the same soul that may have been on Earth, Mars, or other places unknown to us. Could I trace my DNA to these places? No. Is it possible for my cell memory to recall such an experience in a dream or during hypnosis? Yes, that seems to be the case.

Another fact, which has been given repeatedly over the years, is that *each soul has a planet of origin*—what we would consider its *permanent residence*. When our soul was created we each were given choices of where to live, our talents and gifts, and so forth. Some souls choose never to leave the side of Creator. Others choose to live on a specific planet and not leave. Others may live briefly on a planet to fill a special need. For souls that choose to accelerate spiritual growth, they may get permission to leave their planet and come to the Earth, the current "Planet of Learning." Whatever the *planet of origin* of a soul, that soul goes through a process of getting required prior approval to leave that planet and prior approval to enter the desired other planetary system. As I understand it, this is part of a long and serious process of planning and decision-making. And for a soul to enter another planetary system—as a resident—just to experience a life on that planet, the applicant must enter by the "birth route" that planet has in place. (I am reminded that Elijah once said he had spent so many lives as male that he had to go spend time on Venus as a female, because he needed to balance).

The more questions I've asked, the more answers I have received, which I find amazing and humbling. On February 11, 2011, I was given such information after I explained to Naomi my understanding of how things work on what we call the Other Side. On this day, I had shared with Naomi how I had been researching works of various authors and feel that *most are searching for God everywhere outside, not inside, themselves.* Some have spent years of travel seeking and questioning others. Some have spent years in the field of molecular biology and other areas searching aspects of cell structure and cell behavior, or lack of behavior, in response to different stimuli and different environments. I, on the other hand, have mainly received channeling about the Other Side and asked questions. I am amazed at the material channeled through Naomi. I often feel that the *channeled material fills the "gaps in information" that researchers seek. Few mention Creator or God in the research and most do not mention channeled information.*

Naomi commented that she had a client recently who was disturbed by a dream she had of another life she had lived somewhere. In that life, she clearly saw herself and knew that she was seeing herself. However, she said that her physical form was very strange. She had large *eyes and spindly extremities*. She felt that she looked almost like what we call *insects*. Since Naomi does not recall what she channels, she asked me if she had channeled anyone described like that. I answered not that I recall. However, on the Internet, I have seen pictures of beings that are described as *Reptilian groups* and *Mantis groups*, among others. These are alleged to be beings from other planetary systems that some humans say they have seen. I have not personally seen anyone. I have been shown a few beings in dreams and none were mean or threatening. I told Naomi that some that have channeled have said that if we saw them in their natural state, we would be frightened. But for us, they do appear to look as we do. *By thought they change their appearance and by thought, they travel.*

Also, I mentioned that I am often confused, when I receive channeling and the words Creator and God are used interchangeably. Now, recently, I've been led to *authors who write of the human being inside—the psyche—dreams, hypnosis and clearing of traumatic memories of the present and past lives.* I told Naomi that—as she works with people who believe—she channels material that helps them release harmful cell memories. So following our lengthy discussion, visitors appeared to Naomi. Usually, Naomi has no clue what I am talking about.

On this particular day, Jamiah and Ma-ka-la came. Jamiah, I have come to know but Makala is new to me. I met her recently when I volunteered to share my session with another person who was seeking assistance. The following is a synopsis of what transpired from my comments to Naomi on this day. The visitors came to clarify my understanding of the Creator energy versus God energy. In essence, it seems to be a matter of energy intensity or energy strength and it is emphasized that where they are, all are equal, and all are cautious in how they describe the Creator, as none are able to adequately do this. Basically, they are all of Creator's energy, and we are all part of Creator's energy, all souls of the White Light are of the Creator's energy.

Elijah, Jamiah and Makala

Elijah appeared to Naomi and said that he was summoned by Creator to escort two very high-level energies to this site to channel. He was honored to be of service to such beings as Jamiah and Makala. Jamiah chose to have

Makala speak. Jamiah has trouble with our language and refuses to use the machine that converts his language to English. He did make it clear that Creator had heard my conversation with Naomi and sent the two of them to clear up any confusion.

First, Jamiah made it clear that he reports to Father God and Makala reports to Mother God. Jamiah also made it clear that Makala is not to be confused with Matrea. Oshinbah we know as a male ambassador that travels among universes. Matrea is the female ambassador in the same position as that of Oshinbah. Jamiah asked that Makala deliver the message that Creator wanted delivered because Jamiah did not understand the "problem of our lack of understanding."

Naomi in repeating the words of Makala spoke softly and very quickly. Makala said: How nice to be with you again. Jamiah bless his sweet soul. First the image of Creator must be clear in your thinking process. The concept of Creator is very difficult to explain to humans on Earth because the brain of humans can only take in that which they have read of or that of which they have knowledge. Now we are speaking of the *brains of you in human form, not your soul.*

If you have a huge globe and it is filled with the highest and purest energy and this globe of pure energy is larger than anything you can possibly imagine. This purest and highest of energy is Creator. There is no contamination in this energy. *When Creator began creating he made Mother God and Father God.*

Now, in creating, Creator also made universes, planetary systems, and galaxies. He placed the planets and planetary inhabitants within these systems. Now, Creator—for the purpose of overseeing the universes or planetary systems—*created Godships for each of the planetary systems.*

In your area, *you call this energy over your planetary system God.* Some souls of your planet call this energy system Buddha and some call it by different names—that mean leadership. Now, Creator made the Godships so that those in that area—whichever planetary system that is—go to that particular God when they pray and make requests or give thanks. Now, on Earth, when your physical expires and your soul is free to come back (home), you first go back to the sphere of God over the Earth planetary system. Very rarely do you ever go to the Creator. You may go in talking to Creator but you are, more or less, going to what you might call immediate supervisor of that earthly journey. That is how the Godships were formed. Do your understand?

I restated my understanding. Imagine a globe that is filled with Creator's energy. Creator made all of the universes, all of the galaxies, and all of the planetary systems and placed them in this gigantic globe—in that energy field. All that he made only filled a fraction of the globe. So, Creator was part of what he created and still had vast unlimited energy left and continued to create. Then Creator made Godships and placed them—one God—over each planetary system.

Makala answered: Correct. It can be very complicated if you allow—as you were speaking earlier about the scientists trying to find God, so it is with the energy. *You may be going around it, over it, or above it. That is why I am trying to simplify.*

Your friend Elijah once explained how a soul could choose to splinter. As an illustration, he used what he called the octopus effect. Let me use the octopus to help you understand this concept. Think of the octopus head as Creator. Then let each tentacle represent the different creations. *First a very large tentacle would be Father God, which represents all that is masculine energy. Another huge tentacle* would be Mother God, which represents all *that is of the feminine energy.*

Then there would be several different tentacles and each of these tentacles would represent each of the Gods over each of the universes or planetary systems—whichever Creator calls them. At the end of the tentacles then are the soul inhabitants of the planetary systems.

My main goal is to break it down so that you can understand. We do not call it a delegation system because we are all equal. We are very careful how we describe this. There is just more energy for a defined purpose of the masculine Father God and the same applies with feminine Mother God. Now, as Jamiah is to Father God, I am to Mother God. I know you have a question.

Grace: Thank you. The energy of Creator is it also masculine and feminine? Makala: It is neither; it is neutral. It is the most powerful of energy. There is no comparison of that isolate energy that is Creator. The energy that is Creator is greater than all other energy combined. That gives Creator abilities to make more souls to do whatever is necessary. Again, understand, it is pure energy. It is not contaminated.

As Jamiah dozes into a state of peace, he does not like to explain this, and he does not know why humans on earth do not understand this. I, as the loving, compassionate side of femininity—understand and know that in the soul, you do understand. Once the soul inhabits an enclosure it no longer has a memory of this.

By the way, your friend Elijah and I are very close now, as travelers. I do traveling with him. I am doing more of that now because it is the desire of Creator that—before Earth expires—to reverse the masculinity, the control the earth has been under, but not go to pure femininity but to have equality between the two. That is why, Creator asked that I come to Earth more and do more speaking to all of you. The final changes are supposed to embrace femininity but allow the masculine to exist also. That is probably why Jamiah is resting because he has been on duty, on call, for all these eons. Do you have anything else? I said no.

May 6, 2011, I spoke to Naomi of my frustrations in completing the book. I expressed my desire to use the material given by Makala recently but that I was not sure if she meant for me to place that material in the book. She might have been just answering my questions.

Naomi barely had time to respond when Elijah came. He obtained permission from Creator to come for a short visit, and also, to escort Makala safely to this area. Makala promptly appeared. She stated that she knows of my concerns and Creator summoned her to come and clarify any uncertainty.

Makala said for the purposes of being plain and simple so that all will be clearly understand, the Creator is neutral energy but also addressed as Mother God and Father God. Bear with me, because it could become confusing—from that—Jamiah and I serve.

Then we have, as you stated, the *Godships—a God of each universe* or planetary system—or whatever our Creator tells us. Under the *Godship again, there is Mother God and separately, there is Father God. So you have it two times. We, Jamiah and I, serve the primary Creator, but we also help the Mother God and the Father God of the Godship. When I say help, it is as assisting,* just as I am assisting you today. Theirs is like requesting that we be there when they are not quite sure of their major role in what to do. So, we advise. We do not just advise—we represent Creator—so, we must be very careful in our choices.

I asked Makala: Would you and Jamiah be like "go-betweens?" Would you go between the planetary inhabitants and the God of that planetary system, and between the God over the planetary system and the Creator?

Makala replied: Correct. *Print it as such.* There have been many discussions and many authors have printed what they feel is correct. *Very few times has this information—just given to you—been written about in the correct form. Many of the authors write of the Creator and Mother God, which is correct. But they do not speak of a Godship or a Mother God or Father God under that because no one has requested—as you have—for a higher energy to come and explain.* It is what they have received, perhaps from spirit guides and that was correct information, it just was not complete with the status of others all the way through.

That information I gave last time, I believe I did state not to quote me. *Creator said that I should instead ask you to reveal this for clarity since others have not. I really must go.* Do you have anything else?

I said, since you already know the contents of this book, I would appreciate your comments. Makala answered, there are many brilliant and prominent authors on Earth who are messengers to the others of the world. Some travel the world and write on a high medical/ scientific plane and some write so the average person may understand and benefit. Yours is of the latter, reviewing some of the famous material and converting that and the channeling to the understanding of other human brains.

With regard to clearing cell memory and removing the scar patterns of the soul, (that is) we call holding onto the negative thoughts feeding the dark energy. When you repeat the same thought—I have a stomach problem, or other problem—you are declaring it. *Instead, say: I no longer have the problem. It has been replaced by Creator's love. Your many medical problems are first created by being contaminated and your eating of artificial foods. Another problem is the dark energy having access to the thought process and manipulating the thoughts to the point you claim the illness and process.*

Authors speak and write of these things and *people hear and read but do not act* upon what they read. If people would practice it, the disease would leave, not exist. Most go right back to and keep repeating the same thoughts and *the condition regenerates.*

Are you aware of what hypnosis does? It speaks to the soul It goes directly to the soul and gives to the subconscious and all working parts of the body that message. It is amazing. People scoff at hypnosis. They have doubts. But, the reason people have doubts is they hear all and know all because they rarely go into a deep sleep. In hypnosis, they feel that nothing is occurring but it is happening. They release.

Also, *you are correct about your thoughts on near-death-experiences. They are charted options to exit.*

Now, I really must go. You do not need my permission or that of Creator to write of these things, go with your feelings, if we are not available. I rarely come like this. End.

2

Naomi and Cell Memory Work

Through Naomi, Athena, my Spirit Guide, requested that I emphasize these facts: *Cell memory* is *the essence of the soul. Soul cell memory is carried forward each lifetime.* When the soul occupies a vehicle—such as the human body, or a form made of different compositions on other planetary systems—the soul manifests and the cell memory is born again also. The same soul exists throughout eternity. The soul DNA and cell memory are eternal. Like an advertisement, this is repeated so it is remembered.

Cell memories are recordings of events in our lives that are positive and helpful and also those that are negative and traumatic. We *retain our intellect,* our personality and things learned from each life. So it is advisable to learn as much as possible of things that are helpful to soul growth and that sustain physical health. We also may retain and bring forth cell memories of the negative and traumatic. These are the ones that usually cause the most damage to our soul growth and general health. These are the painful emotions of abuse, betrayal, or physical trauma that cause great pain. It is possible to bring these memories forth and release them. Thereafter, healing of the soul occurs.

There is no magic bullet that addresses all cell memory problems. Channeled material states that it is important to bring problem issues to the conscious level and release them. Some people may release problems by just talking to a trustworthy friend. Sometimes people talk with nurses about sensitive issues. Others see social workers for counseling and guidance. Many seek the professional services of a psychiatrist. Some psychiatrists perform regressive hypnosis, as well as counseling. This has been shown to be effective in clearing not only a cell memory problem, but also, the health problem related to the cell memory. The following paragraphs confirm the value of "talk therapy."

Deepak Chopra, M.D., in his book *Life After Life*, presented this interesting fact: Obsessive-compulsive patients sometimes seek relief through talk therapy instead of Prozac therapy. The results of such choices had not been studied until recently. Using MRI and PET scans, it was discovered that "the same impaired regions that become more normal with Prozac also become more normal with talk therapy. (Deepak Chopra 2006)

Three scientists, Henry Stappy, theoretical physicist, Jeffrey Schwartz, a neuropsychiatrist, and Mario Beauregard, a psychologist, crossed disciplines to develop a workable theory of "quantum mind" that "may revolutionize how mind and brain relate to each other. Central to their theory is 'neuroplasticity,' the notion that brain cells are open to change, flexibly responding to will and intention." Ibid.

"They acknowledge that the usual scientific explanation the 'the mind is what the brain does,' but that this explanation has many flaws. They propose, therefore, that the opposite is true. Mind is the controller of the brain. In their view, the mind is like an electron cloud surrounding the nucleus of an atom. Until an observer appears, electrons have no physical identity in the world; there is only the amorphous cloud. In the same way, imagine that there is a cloud of possibilities open to the brain at every moment (consisting of words, memories, ideas, and images, it could choose from). When the mind gives a signal, one of these possibilities coalesces from the cloud and becomes a thought in the brain, just as an energy wave collapses into an electron. Like the quantum filed generating real particles from virtual ones, the mind generates real brain activity from virtual activity." Ibid.

"What makes this reversal important is that it fits the facts. Neurologists have verified that a mere intention or purposeful act of will alters the brain. Stroke victims, for example, can force themselves, with the aid of a therapist, to use only their right hand if paralysis has occurred on that side of the body. Willing themselves day after day to favor the affected part, they can gradually cause the damaged sites to heal." Ibid.

One of Naomi's many skills is talking to people. She shares stories from her own life and this encourages her clients to also speak freely. Naomi also channels to people that are open to receive or seek information. As Naomi has treated my feet over the years, she simultaneously channeled most of the material for three books. As her gift has become known, more and more people are seeking appointments. Now, she occasionally has Gatherings and channels to a group of people.

Regardless of the type of care a human seeks, the goal is to become healthy in all areas—spiritually, mentally, emotionally and physically and, hopefully, in that order. This corresponds to the advice of Edgar Cayce that first the soul must heal in order for the physical to heal. Also, as given previously, events a soul has charted for this life are things that soul needed and chose to experience for soul growth. *These are soul contracts.* If they are not completed in this lifetime, they must be completed in future life, either on Earth or somewhere else. Cell memory plays a major role in completing this process.

Naomi has had several *clients that proclaimed disbelief* in channeling until they actually experienced it, as she worked on their feet. Afterward, they told her what she said. Such clients are often in tears because the client recognized the one who spoke through Naomi. Occasionally, Naomi shares a story with me but not the names. One such client was a male who deeply cared for his mother. He had to make the decision for doctors to remove artificial life support measures. He later felt guilty. This bothered him emotionally for a long time. Finally, a friend brought him to see Naomi. During his treatment, the soul of his mother thanked him for his decision to let her go. She let him know that her soul is very happy on the Other Side. The man cried and was grateful. His soul was freed of this burden of guilt.

Another case was a woman whose son went camping overnight with few close male friends. They were all around age twenty. They apparently hiked up a hill and pitched their camp on top of a bluff rock. The opposite side of this bluff rock was a cliff. The distance to the ground below was of about a hundred feet. Her son had poor vision and he did not have his usual glasses with him. During the night, he got up and literally walked off the cliff. It was and accident. He could not see where he was going. He died from the fall. A few days or weeks later, his mom came to Naomi and he channeled back to his mother and told her what happened.

A third client lost his wife to a disease. He and his wife had been very close to their daughter and grandchild. The grandchild, a girl, and the grandmother had always spent private time playing with dolls. The child's mother became concerned because, after her mother's death, the child continued to play and speak just like the grandmother was there. The man came to Naomi. At some point, the late wife channeled to the man that on a given day, he would receive a call and be asked to pick-up the child from school. On that day, he would witness the child playing with dolls and know that indeed it was the soul of his wife visiting the child. Also, they were asked to not scold the child or think that something was emotionally wrong with her. The events happened, as the late wife channeled they would.

My own very lengthy period of working with Naomi and Dr. Sigmund Freud helped me work through a lot of cell memory problems. Also, Dr. Freud said that, in other lives, he and I worked in the same field, psychiatry. He said that on the Other Side, I do cell memory clearing. I work with the cases that have the most difficult time clearing cell memory. This work with him is supposed to "help me remember what I already know about cell memory." I have often felt that it was an experiment to see if I would recall, but Dr. Freud said it was not an experiment. *Dr. Freud stated that dreams and hypnosis are two ways to clear traumatic cell memories.*

Now, before proceeding, as promised earlier, I will give instructions for protecting yourself or your loved ones from dark or negative energy. Also, I'll share the technique for recalling dreams. This is channeled information given by Elijah, Cayce, Thomas (the Biblical Doubting Thomas), and many others. This is a simple means of self-protection day-to-day and also, during the many disasters now occurring on Earth.

3

Surrounding Self with Light

This procedure may be done anywhere at anytime. It is advisable to perform this procedure often to protect yourself from dark or negative energy.

It is also advisable that pregnant women use this prayer often to protect themselves and the fetus. Also, the parents, but especially the mother, of an unborn child should also give positive thoughts to the universe, to Creator, about the type of child they desire.

According to souls that have channeled this information, Dark Energies, or those of negative energy try to strike those of White Light when they are off guard, or vulnerable. Examples of vulnerable times would be when you are sick, injured, very tired or emotionally upset.

This is a mental exercise of protection to do at the following times: before bedtime, and upon awakening in the morning; before meeting new people; before making important phone calls and before important conversations. Do this before handling anything of a legal nature or of potential conflict. You may also project the thoughts of protection to loved ones whether or near or far away.

The procedure is simple. Remember: *Mind follows breath, so take a few slow deep breaths to relax.* Be quiet and focus your mind. Use the mind to say to yourself:

> *I surround myself by the White Light of the Holy Spirit for protection from dark/negative energy. Visualize yourself surrounded by pure white light a few inches deep.*

> *State: On top of the White Light of the Holy Spirit, I place the Pink Light of God.*

On top of the Pink Light, I place the Gold Light of the Creator.

On top of all this, I surround myself with reverse mirrors so that any negative or dark energy directed toward me will, instead, return to the sender. End

4

Prepare to Dream

Sylvia Browne, in her book *Dreams,* does not profess to have all the answers about dreams. She shares what she has learned working with her dreams and those of others for over thirty-years. She does state that hers is a life blessed. She is devoted to God, spirituality, and the use of her psychic gifts in whatever ways she can apply them to help others. Sylvia states "that it is fairly common knowledge now that there are two basic stages of sleep: REM, which stands for 'rapid eye movement' and is the lightest stage of sleep, and Non-REM, which is the deeper sleep when eye movements and our other muscle responses become almost nonexistent. It is during REM sleep that we dream, and it's when we're awakened during or immediately after REM sleep that we're most likely to remember our dreams. (Sylvia Browne 2002)

Research indicates that "successful sleep depends upon the natural balance and flow of the REM and the Non-REM cycles, and the various levels of brain wave activity, I can't stress enough how I hope that, unless it's prescribed by a qualified doctor, you'll resist the temptation to medicate yourself with drugs or alcohol to help yourself sleep." . . . Experts and researchers have proven that alcohol and sleep medications disrupt the balance of your sleep cycles. Such imbalances may result in no dreams at all or dreams that are bizarre like a house of mirrors. When you wake up, you may feel hungover or emotionally flat. Ibid.

Sylvia expressed that she has "no doubt in her mind that dreaming is as essential to us as breathing. Whether we remember our dreams or not, whether we can even begin to understand what they mean, they're a release valve, an absolute survival mechanism, our minds' way of protecting and preserving some sense of balance in a waking world that often seems to offer very little balance at all . . . . Dreams are so necessary that in clinical studies it's been found that after several nights of REM deprivation, the first thing the mind and body will do when allowed to sleep uninterrupted is indulge in a dramatic increase in the length and frequency of REM cycles to make up for lost time. They are so necessary that without them, we can experience everything in the cold light of day from disorientation to an inability to concentrate or be logical to anxiety to depression to hallucinations—in other words, those often disquieting indulgences we can freely express in private while we sleep."Ibid

Sylvia lists five types of dreams categories and says that every dream experience is one of these five kinds:

The Prophetic Dream—has two qualities in common. It is always in color, never black and white. And the action in the dream takes place in a sequence of logical order. The prophetic dreams originate in the detailed charts we made on the other side. These include likes, dislikes, our family members, our exits points we planned as options and so forth. Ibid.

The Release Dream—is a good news/bad news scenario. The bad news is they are rarely enjoyable because we rarely feel the need to release things in our lives that we are happy and content about. The release dreams are "to bring unresolved or unexpected issues into a spotlight and subconsciously act our whatever frustrations, anger, regret, guilt, resentment, betrayal, embarrassment, or shame we've been lugging around." Ibid.

The Wish Dream—is usually about what we want or think we want. Deeper probing into the dream may reveal something we perceive as missing pieces emotionally or spiritually in our lives. Ibid.

The Information or Problem-Solving Dream—Sylvia states that there are greater and higher sources at work around us all the time waiting for us to give them access. She lists many famous people who received their brilliant ideas in dreams: Mozart, Einstein, Elias Howe, Thomas Edison, Robert Louis Stevenson and Dr. Jonas Salk to name a few. Ibid.

Astral Visits—Sylvia says that astral travel is simply our spirits taking a break from the confines of these limited, cumbersome, gravity-challenged bodies and traveling to whomever or wherever we want.

Like telepathy, astral travel is natural. It is an innate God-given talent. It was astral travel that brought our souls here from the Other Side, and it is astral travel that will take us back to the Other Side, our home, when we leave the physical body. We are born knowing how to astral travel and we routinely do this. It is at the core of many of our most vivid dreams. Ibid.

(The above five kinds of dreams are chapter titles in Sylvia's book *Dreams*. In each chapter, she defines the kind of dream and discusses and gives examples of the specific dream category).

Sylvia Browne praised the "fascinating work of Carl Jung, who was one of the greatest psychologists of the twentieth century. He devoted a great deal of his life to dreams, their symbolism and their overall importance in our lives. In his book *On the Nature of Dreams*, published in 1945, Jung described an approach he called "taking up the context." That means that in order to fully decipher the meaning of the symbols in dreams, we have to take our own 'context,' or personal associations with those symbols, into account." In other words, when you dream about a symbol such as a house or a bird, what does the house or bird mean to you. Sylvia says learn all you can about dreams and then toss it out. The important thing is what the dream means to you.

From channeling, we know that all people dream. Dreams are one way of bringing stored memories to the surface so they can be recognized and released. Dreams are another way of working through problems on the Other Side and assessing our progress in this life. Dreams are activities of the mind/brain at work during sleep. They sort, assess, coordinate, and file events of the waking state with those of the unconscious state. The soul is the permanent storage area for the events of the day. At the end of each day, the soul updates its records with events experienced that day. The hurtful, traumatic, and negative events get filed along with the happy experiences. Understand this, if the soul has cleared a traumatic memory, it is erased in the soul memory, and it is cleared in the Hall of Records.

Events that are painful tend to remain like a wound to the soul. They also remain as painful memories in the conscious mind. Even if you able to put them out of your mind temporarily, something will trigger their recurrence. These memories are the ones we call "baggage" waiting to be unloaded. If they are not unloaded, they may manifest as emotional or physical illness. They nudge and gnaw at us during the waking state. In the sleep state, they may cause restlessness and nightmares, as our inner self seeks solutions.

To recall dreams:

Place a pad of paper and pen beside your bed.

Quiet the mind by taking slow deep breaths.

Place the lights around yourself.

Then say to yourself, I will awake and record what I dream. This statement made while you are awake, says to your unconscious self, your soul, pay attention and wake me when I have completed my dream.

(Of course, if your guide is like Elijah or Athena, you may be awakened by what sounds like a doorbell, a cell phone, or you may hear your name called).

At first, you may only recall one word or one image. Whatever you recall write it down. In a short time, you will start to recall more and more. Record all that you remember. If you recall dress style, colors, houses, or cars, record what you saw. These give you insight as to the possible year of the setting. For example: Were people wearing modern clothing styles or were they perhaps Victorian styles or military styles. What was the main activity? How did you feel in the dream? Were you an observer or participant? What were you doing? Were you alone? Who did you see? If known, what does the person mean to you?

You learn a great deal about yourself by working with your dreams. If you don't have someone gifted in dream interpretation, you can read many books on the subject. I personally learned a lot about dreams from the books of Edgar Cayce and Sylvia Browne. Dreams are filled with symbols and, as you work with dreams, you begin to recognize what they mean to you. For example, I now recognize when I am on the Other Side. For me, these dreams appear as very quiet, peaceful settings. There usually is a lot of light. At times, there are vivid beautiful colors of sky, beaches, plants or buildings. There is a logical sequence in these dreams and I awaken feeling refreshed and peaceful.

If you have relatives that have crossed to the Other Side (physically died), they may appear to you in soul form and appear to be the age when you last saw them so you will recognize them or they may appear younger. They will communicate by thought, so don't expect to hear a big hello and a big conversation. Expect instead to feel love, peace, and happiness from them. They may have big smiles or show you nice furnished rooms where they now reside. These are just friendly visits and they are showing you that they are happy.

As you work with dreams, you will come to realize which ones are important and which ones are just fragments and mean nothing. End

5

Near Death Experience: Option to Exit

Those of us who have had what is called the *"near death experience"* (NDE) know without doubt that this was not just a dream. We know where we were, what we saw, what we felt and that we communicated by telepathy. I believe what happens is that the soul temporarily leaves the body and has total awareness of its past, present and future. I know that is what happened to me following my concussion on 9/11/1980. I was aware that I was outside of my physical body or "house for my soul." I was aware and very conscious of what was being said to me by thought. I knew that the Presence was the Creator of my soul. I knew I was home. There was no time. There was no fear. It was a natural event. I was told how things are supposed to work and that we have been taught wrong. At the time, I did not understand. (Grace J. Scott 2009)

I believe that—during the NDE the person, the soul, is at some point offered the chance to exit this life. The soul still attached to the physical person may be temporarily confused about the situation. I was. And, in some cases, the soul is informed that it is not his or her time to exit. In my case, I was given a choice.

Briefly, following a work accident, I suffered what was called a "mild concussion." The symptoms were bad. For the first time in my life I was mentally and physically not functioning. Normally, I was high energy and constantly busy. My whole family life was disrupted. My husband and I had a teenage son and a younger daughter. I was home alone a lot as my husband worked and the children were in school. My daughter piled all her stuffed animals on my bed to keep me company and to show she loved me and wanted me to get well. Vicki's teacher called about her schoolwork. Vicki had voiced fears that I would die.

I am leaving out a lot. One night I had a "dream" that was not a dream. It was real. I was out of body and floating toward brilliant white Light. Messages were given to me by telepathy. You have been taught wrong. You are taught not to be selfish. The correct teaching is, be selfless and, at that point, I was shown in the heart area how that feels—a gentle flutter. I was told you are going through a stage of transition. It will be lonely at first. Around this time, I was shown my life. It was from the time my youngest sister was a baby lying on a blanket on the grass of our front yard. My next sister was around age two and standing beside her. I was about age 6 wondering where my mother was and why she left me to care for these two babies. Next I was shown my young teen years and the little things about which I felt guilt based on our Church of Christ teachings. Each frame appeared like a picture screen or slide show and each was waved aside as no problem.

I was told that the most important thing is to stay connected to the Creator. I was told that just as each grain of sand makes up the beach, each soul is a particle of light of the Creator. I remember a ray of light as an example of souls being particles of Light. I felt like I was being held gently in the palm of a hands placed together. This Presence was of something massive and indescribable but also totally filled with pure love and gentleness. There was total love, total peace, total joy and total acceptance. All I saw was beautiful blue color like the sky. I never wanted to leave this Presence. Simultaneously, I was given the choice. Once you enter the Light there is no turning back. The Light was pure white. The choices are yours. I thought choices what choices. At that second, I said: What about my husband and children? With that thought, I felt like I was slammed back into my body. I sat up in my bed totally shocked and in awe.

Later I realized that one doubt caused my soul to return to the body. Thereafter, I had extra-sensory-perception for several months. Also, one day, following mood swings and crying, I gazed into a mirror trying to understand what was happening to me. Suddenly, I felt split, like there was someone beside me that was also part of me but I did not know that person. Right after that, there was no reflection in the mirror. That scared me! I called a psychiatrist. She determined that I had been traumatized, was depressed, and had not mourned my mother's death. I was not losing my mind. That was good news. I gradually recovered with the support of my family and doctors, a diet with no additives or stimulants and drinking lots of water. I slept most of the time. I read a lot. But this was a traumatic event in one sense, and a blessing in another sense. I never looked at death, and religion the same after that. Ibid.

Flash forward to the present 2011. Another 9/11 brought down the World Trade Centers in 2001 and delivered the souls Elijah, Alan, Angelo, Athena, Oshinbah, Edgar Cayce, Celonious and others to me through channeling. I realize that my NDE was an option I had charted to exit. But the blessing in it was I no longer feared death. Also, another blessing has been that it is easy for me to accept the channeling. And more recently, in 2010, another personal event occurred. My uncle who was on ventilator contacted me through Naomi and my spirit guide just before and just after his death. This is what happened.

My uncle had gradually deteriorated over the last ten years. He had often told me that his greatest fear was to become mentally incompetent, as his father and two of his siblings had done. He also said his mental status was never the same following open-heart surgery, which he described in detail. His primary caregiver was his wife. Their six children were involved in their careers and families, for the most part. (I had been an extension of the family for about two years when I was age twenty-one and fresh out of a Catholic hospital school of nursing). One of their daughters that lived a few doors away was most involved in the day-to-day care and back-up plan when needed.

When I retired and returned to my roots, he was the first to recognize how lost I felt and how foreign this town felt after thirty plus years in New York City. On one trip south—while staying with them and looking for a house—he took me to a little farm he owned to pick a watermelon for dinner. When we arrived he said nothing. He just observed. He knew that I would see an old mule leaning over a fence to be petted and walk in the dirt and through the weeds of an overgrown garden. He knew my dad's pair of mules—Maude and Kate—and how—as a child—his life and mine had been on the same family farm. Mules worked hard and helped sustain the gardens for human food and the fields of food for the animals.

Now, in 2010, his very strong wife/caretaker was worn out caring for him and became terminally ill and confused. He, meanwhile, had been physically healthy but mentally confused for some time. Both were admitted to a Long Term Care Facility nearby. After a few months, he suddenly developed pneumonia and was admitted to the hospital.

At some point he was placed on a ventilator because the children were told he had a chance to recover. This led to his channeling to me through Naomi. He clearly stated his name and asked that I give his children the following message, which I've condensed. The souls of your mother and I are already on the Other Side most of the time. Remove all this equipment and let me go. It is time for me to go. I contacted the children and did tell them the message. Of course I had to explain about working with channeling and the two books, which I had not mentioned. Plus, I had been working with them for a few months about nursing home care, death and dying. Even though three of the six children are pharmacists, none had experience with hands on care or personal experience with death.

Within a week, the life support system was removed, as he requested. I was with family members for emotional support when this was done. My uncle breathed without assistance for about four hours and then quietly died physically. His funeral was scheduled for late afternoon a couple of days later. On the morning of his funeral, I went to Naomi. My uncle again sent a message for the family. My guide Athena had been in the cleansing area and my uncle insisted that she bring to me the message he gave to her. He stated his full name and the message title: This is "full name" From the Beyond." He stated that he was very happy where he is, that he had a wonderful life and grew spiritually because of his wife and children. The experience of being the husband and father to those in his life was one of growth and very important. He gave praise for his children and for his wonderful and talented grandchildren.

Also, he acknowledged my role in his life and that he, his wife, and I had charted to be together, as we had been. He also stated that we had been supportive of each other in other life times. I remembered he always said to me on different occasions—"you would be helping us and we would be helping you." Also, he said he had not been aware that I had written books until he crossed over. Now, he is aware and very proud of the fact. He approved of the books and said he felt the children would be helpful in their sales. When he closed, he again spoke: This is "full name" From the Beyond.

My husband and I worked fast and accomplished what he requested. The children had no spare time to read the material before the funeral. But they did do it after the burial service. They got together in private and read the material. They expressed their gratitude.

My uncle came through again and requested that the children let their mother go. He also asked that I speak with her. He wanted me to tell her that all was well and that he was waiting to assist her across. I did. She smiled faintly and nodded that she understood. Later, it was given that she did not understand why I told her that because leave is what she had been trying to do but was pulled back each time. A few weeks later, my aunt died. My uncle channeled that they were now in the same building where the Chambers for cleansing are located. Each one is going through the cleansing process. After the cleansing—as a team—they will participate in the Earth changes. They will be part of a team of souls assisting other souls that cross over during the cataclysmic events to come. This was a charted part of their mission.

I believe that in the cases of the NDE, channeling, or hypnosis that the "veil" lifts and we access the records of our soul's origin and the soul's history. The veil consisting of time and religion are lifted.

Dr. Raymond Moody coined the phrase "near death experience" (NDE). He documented cases of people who had the experience. The amazing part that connected them was their descriptions of what they described, what they saw, what they learned, how they felt. It was through reading his book *Life after Life* when I was injured in 1980 that I figured out what had happened to me when I had a concussion. I think a similar thing happens on some level of the mind when material is channeled and when people undergo hypnosis or do deep meditation.

Channeled information has stated that the ancients knew how to work with the soul and help people change their lives. For example, in times of stress or episodes of severe pain the ancients knew how to pull the soul from the body through meditation. *The body does not feel pain when the soul is not present—when the soul is able to rise from the body.* In other words, in deep meditation, the soul is able to increase its vibration and rise out of the body, yet remain attached to the body. We've been advised that when we have stress or experience a traumatic event—such as disasters on Earth—to go into an altered state of consciousness through meditation. This is a protective state for the soul, a turning inside to God, to our Creator.

Naomi does a similar thing when she channels. I call it an altered state. She suddenly senses an energy approaching. The energy may be strong or weak. She often describes what she feels and sees as the energy approaches. She then focuses her attention to an area to her front and right several inches. The energy then manifests to her a "physical appearance" that she identifies and describes. Also, she states if they appear serious or jovial. She usually says that she senses their kindness, love or compassion. Even for the other planetary visitors, they explain that they manifest their appearance for our emotional comfort and acceptance. Some say that if we actually saw their real appearance we might be frightened. Naomi however, always looks at their eyes and feels their love and compassion. I believe that Naomi and those who do hypnotic regressions and progressions are working with the same levels of the mind, subconscious or soul.

6

Organ Transplants: Issues and concerns

I pondered the writing of this section, I felt that I needed more information and spoke of this to Naomi. I had a mental-block. I was stuck. She asked me numerous questions about things she has channeled but does not recall and refuses to read. As I spoke, this helped. Then later Elijah came and channeled the name of someone I needed to meet. I acted on his advice and within days we did meet. The person provided the reference material that I needed and suggested others. In addition, we had lunch and spent a few hours talking. I felt like she was a walking library of information and experience on social work, heart transplants, hypnosis, meditation, near-death experiences and other subjects.

Among the books recommended and read was *Transplant* by Dr. William Frist who started the Heart and Heart-Lung Transplant Program at Vanderbilt Hospital. I became informed not only about the problems faced by transplant patients but the stress experienced by their caregivers—families, physicians and nurses. The patients awaiting transplants are living between two worlds, life or death. Usually by the time they need a transplant they are very sick and this is the "last-ditch" effort to survive. The patient and family have concerns of how to pay for the procedure, physician fees, medications, and how much or if their insurance will pay. Originally, the procedure was not covered. Now, more insurance providers do cover portions of the procedure and part of medication costs. Another major expense is ongoing doctor visits and procedures following the transplant. Again, these may or may not be covered depending upon the patient's insurance policy.

A big concern of the patient and the health care workers is that the patient's body will reject the organ. Cells of the patient's body recognize the donated organ as foreign and the immune system attacks it. The only treatment option to prevent rejection is immunosuppressive drugs for life. Often, additional other drugs are also required. Of these, some are antibiotics to prevent or treat infections, and others are to treat symptoms caused by the required drugs. Some patients have reactions to the required drugs and this is uncomfortable. Dr. Frist pointed out that—like his father before him—he relied heavily on reports by nurses who provided care around the clock. Nurses were very sensitive to the mental and emotional status of patients and families. Nurses were very tuned in to physical signs and symptoms of early rejection. Often, it was the observations and reports of nurses that prompted immediate performance of tests for organ rejection. Signs of rejection were very hard on the patient, families and staff.

Hotel costs are another expense for the patient and family. The patient and family may be required to stay in a hotel on standby waiting to see if the anticipated heart is the proper match. After the surgery the patient must remain near the hospital for a specific length of time depending upon the patient's condition.

The doctors and nurses have specific stresses also. The doctors have to make hard decisions about the available organ and which patient has the best chance of surviving with the heart. The lead doctor gets little free time to rest or be with family. He or she is up and running to procure an organ at whatever hour the need arises. At the same time, the doctor must be highly attuned to all steps in the process: This includes procuring the heart at a far away hospital, transporting the heart to the hospital where the recipient is waiting, removal of the recipients own heart and inserting the donor heart. Doctors, nurse, social workers, anesthesiologists, respiratory staff, laboratory staff and others are all required and part of the team to successfully perform a transplant. All work long hours and many try not to become attached to the patient. Being too close may impede objective decisions. There were no comments in the book as to whether patients with new hearts reported changes in personality or food preferences. Overall, this book was very informative and I learned a lot. (Also, in a sense, the book took me back to memories of my years as a student when I knew an elderly Dr. Frist when he made rounds. Indeed, he too was a special doctor).

7

The Beyond: Transplants and Cell Memory

As a *follow-up to the organ transplant topic*, I asked in my session with Naomi why some patients report cell memory issues and others do not. Critics on the Internet try to deny the existence of cell memory transfer because it does not always occur. The entity that responded did not give a name. The following statements were given 1/14/2011.

"The answer to that is everyone does have the cell memory transfer from donor to recipient. The recipient denies it. The recipient goes into denial. They feel they are not connected to the organ. Their emotional/ mental self, their brain process, cannot handle what they heard. The organ is not malfunctioning. They are in denial.

They know they will have the same cell memory transfers as those who speak of it but they do not admit it. Instead they bury the memories. Now, let me speak of this. When they go into denial and do not speak of the cravings, the desires or whatever they feel or the unusual happenings, then they have to deal with that when they cross over. They have created another cell memory. Now, the problem with denial and burying the memories is that you come over here and have to cleanse them.

Ninety percent of organ transplant recipients do have the experience of cell memory transfer from the donor organ. They have the same feelings their donor had but they do not speak of it. They know it. They may write it down. They do not acknowledge it publicly. That does not mean that they do not have it.

If scientists or doctor go and question these transplant recipients, they will frighten the recipients and they will not give them the information that they know they have. The reason is that they do not want their names in a public paper, in a study or a test result. They don't want their private life invaded. So, they will not tell the doctors and scientist what is really happening.

We wanted you to know this. We on this side keep a record also and it is ninety percent or higher. The recipients deny all of it. They don't want to talk about. They don't want to go public. Some are frightened of it and afraid to go public and some are afraid they will be criticized or ridiculed and not believed. As we stated, they are creating more cell memories. If they don't deal with it on Earth, then they will have to deal with it when they cross over to where we are. Then if they don't clear, then in their next life they will be carrying that with them. This means then they have to experience another organ donor so they will express this.

You see, the organ donor—the recipient receiving a body part of another person is important for scientific research. Not coming forth thwarts the research that could benefit all.

I asked about the case of the patient who was unhappy with heart transplant. The Other Side commented: This case is to let the public realize that not all cases are smooth. The heart keeps the body alive and breathing. She was chosen on this side to present another side of awareness. There should have been a caution in her book that this was my experience; it may not be your experience.

When a person is born with a problem they adjust to it as they grow. But when you begin substituting parts, then you are getting into another field. This book puts out the question to the general public: Is it worth it? Would it be better to go ahead and cross over to the Other Side or is this what you want to experience? This is what happens when a society advances. This is not of our side and it is not of the Creator."

Enos

On March 18, 2011, I spoke to Naomi about what I am learning about organ transplants and cell memory. I've heard of two cases that refused immunosuppressive drugs and their bodies did not reject the organ. The cases were from the country of India. Suddenly, Naomi announced, we have a visitor. He did not identify himself until the end of the session.

"The whole lesson of organ transplants and cell memory—or a big portion of it or a big impact of it—is that it is teaching souls of every nationality to accept others. In other words, the Creator created each of us. So, if you are in denial of another human—as being equal to you or as being of God, as you are, then you may have a problem if you get an organ transplant. The people of India accept other people. They accept and understand reincarnation.

They understand that in another life they may have lived in England, the United States or elsewhere. They also understand that they may have been a different culture, different race, and different religion. They also understand that the soul may live several lives simultaneously, meaning in the same time frame. Their belief system allows them to accept anything that is foreign to their body.

The whole lesson behind the transplant or the cell memory, or a portion of the cell memory, is for humans to realize that this may have come from a different type of individual but we all are of the Creator in the soul. The soul knows that we are all from the Creator and can accept it and that is where the people of India differ. They do accept. They may not call it Creator but they do accept that all are created equal.

So, the acceptance of an organ and the success of it staying with you depend upon the soul knowing that all souls are equal. The Creator made all souls and all souls are equal. Let's use the example of cars: The past history of the United States includes three major automakers. You had one called Ford. So, if you have five Fords and they are all have the same engine made by the same company. They are made alike in the basic form, but the whole vehicle is not identical. The basics parts are alike. So, you may take a part off of one vehicle and place it into another. The same applies to the human body. They are not all alike but the basic pattern of the human body is the same. So, the acknowledgement of the human soul—that resides in a human body that they are all basically alike—says okay, this organ came from another body but we are all made in the image of the Creator, and we are all made alike. The only thing that I need to do is to accept that which is given to me and know that the characteristics, the patterns and the memories come with it and not be shocked by that.

All I need to do is go with the flow. If this heart, or this kidney gives the message to my brain that I like to ride in airplanes instead of cars, then

I will adjust to it. That is where the people of India have an advantage or upper hand on the rest. They agree and understand. There are other nationalities that are also aware and understand like that. Some of them you may not even know about. They accept that which is. They trust Creator and have acknowledgement of Creator to the point that they are in agreement. They have already determined that they understand that maybe this human body expired for the purpose of going home and its parts being used to assist other people. So, they acknowledge, they are grateful and they understand.

We are talking primarily about India—they also do not think that when death occurs that is the end. They know that the soul will be coming back into another body, another human body. They do not view death as an end, an eternal thing, when you get placed in the ground or whatever.

The main message is that for humans to grow in the spiritual and return back to the Creator—they should—and we emphasize they should—acknowledge and accept that the human form was made by the Creator and no two are alike—not even identical twins are alike. But even though no two are alike, they are still alike in the fact they have like basic parts. They have like basic parts.

Another illustration I wish to use is this. In the South, where you now live, people eat biscuits. They are made from dough. If you roll the dough out, it is the same basic form. If you decided to add cheese to one biscuit, bacon to another and so forth, you still have the basic dough. This is what we are emphasizing—the basics.

Stay with the basics of knowing that each human body was created alike. Then if the transplant or organs are moved from one body to another body it is the acceptance of the receiving soul that makes the difference. If only the soul that is going to receive would acknowledge, appreciate, and accept that the one that donated had decided to return home and it was okay to receive. This would make a difference. Some recipients have a guilt feeling about receiving. They feel that someone had to die for them to receive the organ, which is true except—that individual that crossed over—had chosen that time to cross over.

For that donor, for that person, their goal was to benefit other humans by donating their organs. It was an honor and tribute to their being *selfless*, not selfish, but *selfless* in that they were thinking of others. It gives opportunities for those who are going to cross over to still—not live, but their patterns, characteristics, habits, etc., may still exist in the receiver of that organ—but they know the soul has gone on. All that exists—in the cell memory now from the donor—are the characteristics, habits, and familiarity of events that the original body had. It carries over to the recipient body because it is absorbed in the cells.

Grace: How is the soul separated? Enos answered: The soul is separated as any other soul is separated. It is energy. It is energy and it returns to the Other Side and the energy acknowledges that it assisted another body to survive. This gives the soul a little more—vibrational level—or what you on Earth call level one, two, three, four, and five. The donation assists the soul that donated have a higher energy level. It is like added points for the soul.

Now, you may not have heard this before. The souls that we speak of receiving and giving, before their coming to the Earth, it was already a "done deal." They have arranged, they know that x is going to deplete an organ and y will donate an organ. It is like x needs the organ and y says, I am returning home. Take my organ and complete your journey. We, as a collective, do not know if anyone has brought this forth to you.

I said no, no one has stated this information before. What keeps coming up in the research of the books I've read is about the cell itself. Enos said: The composition of the cell is a unique pattern developed by the body that carried it. That is why it transfers to the other individual. The pattern of the behavior of the other human body is what is stored in the cell. It is transferred to whoever is the recipient of the organs. If no one receives the organ, of course, it leaves.

My name is not a known entity to you. I am on the Other Side as a researcher. I have never been to the planetary systems. I chose to remain on this side. That is why Creator asked that I come and speak with you. Of all the souls that Creator made, there are a few of us who never elected to go anywhere but to assist those who have gone on their journeys. A name is not necessary for me. I exist because Creator made me also. My chosen field is to continue assisting, and at this time, you on the planet Earth have a desire to learn of cell memory, DNA, and cell composition. This is my area of expertise.

Grace: We have researchers that keep looking for the soul in the cell. Enos said: The soul absorbs the characteristics, the memory, from the cell and the soul itself is energy. The soul has the adaptability to go into any form that it requests. For example, if the soul is going to another planet—one on which your human form could not exist because of the chemical makeup of the planet—the soul may enter a rock, a tree, or an inanimate object. They have a reason to go into those. By doing that, you would not need cell memory. You are not doing anything. In those instances, the soul has or carries the cell memory but does not choose to use it. Now, that is a far out example.

Souls, once they have inhabited a planet such as Earth or another planetary system, they usually do not inhabit an inanimate object. If a soul chooses to inhabit an inanimate object, then the soul does so in the very beginning, before the soul ever experiences being in a form. There would be no cell memory in an inanimate object. It is not a breathing object. The soul is there to learn and experience.

This can become very complex. You could be challenged if others cannot accept or have the soul energy level to accept that a soul could inhabit an inanimate object. This could be a challenging event they could put to you, if that ever happened or comes up. Remember what has been stated. *Inanimate objects do not need cells.* They are composed of structure, meaning that if you ever had chemistry—all the minerals and such that make up a composition is what the inanimate objects have. They do not need a soul to be there. But a soul may enter because the soul needs to just experience what it is like to be there, to exist. There is a purpose. I myself, even though I chose to stay here and assist other soul energies, I never felt that I would like to do that. I prefer being active. What it does teach is patience and endurance. There are a lot of positive characteristics that develop when they do that.

There are times when individuals come to a planet—I'll say Earth because you are familiar with Earth—and they are disrespectful to plants, to trees, to living organisms that the Creator has made—when they come back for debriefing—it is not a sentence—it is a selection because the Board doing the review will say: You created harm to the living plant world, to the living creatures, to the living whatever. You may choose to regain and fully redeem your former energy by becoming an inanimate object.

Now, understand, when they elect to do that, it is not a timeframe like you are familiar with. In your time it might be one minute or one hour. But whatever the time, it is long enough for this soul to absorb: You never harm anything that Creator made. You never deliberately put any harm on anything that Creator made. This is a vast, vast, knowledge throughout that you know of before ever going to Earth or know of before going to any other planetary system. But, I would say—percentage wise—one percent may elect to enter an inanimate object. As I stated, it is a result of how they were on other planets, this disrespect and the destruction—if they destroyed. But it does give an immediate solution to allowing the energy to be restored as it once was by choosing to go. Not all choose to do this. Many go all the way back to level one and work their way back up. The fast way is as I stated. Now, I will be returning. There is a soul that is insisting on speaking. He is very strong willed. We need this type of individual to accomplish the deeds that have to be done.

It has been delightful for me to assist you. You do have permission to use any or all the information that I give you. If you wish to quote a soul, you may use the name Enos.

The area in which I reside is like a research lab. There are a few of us there. It is an area by itself that Creator made for us. I have never been on any planetary system.

Grace: Back to the organ transplant patients. In preparing the patient to receive the organ, would it help to train patients to meditate and train them to accept the organ? Enos replied: In your United States there is a lot of erroneous material about religion. Many in your country could not accept what is happening. If they were at a level they could accept, it would help. It would have to be monitored. How much information each individual receives would have to be monitored closely. All who are to receive an organ need to be—not only counseled—but they need to be talked to about the structure and the purpose and the mind acceptance of the organ.

Many in your country, unfortunately, do not believe in reincarnation. Believing in reincarnation makes it much easier. This would help them if they could believe in it. To them, they have been taught that reincarnation is the work of the devil. The approach would have to be taught. The simple answer to your question is that it would help all. Now, I will be in my laboratory. End

8

Connecting the Dots

I was already reading *The Divine Matrix* by Gregg Braden when I was given many additional reference sources. I then bought about ten more books and spent the next few weeks reading. After reading several books and comparing them to channeled material I've received, I was amazed at the similarities in the material. The Gregg Braden book reminds me of the Energy Grids that were been spoken of by Elijah, Edgar Cayce, Oshinbah, aliens and other messengers. I wrote what they gave in *Awakening of the Soul*. A brief synopsis of that follows.

Elijah says that he travels by thought. He thinks of a location and then travels by energy pathways to that location. He travels as fast as he thinks. To reach Naomi, for example, he simply thinks of her and her location. Each of us has an energy pathway that those of other dimensions may use to reach us and monitor us. Eventually, in our future following the Earth axis shift, we also will be able to travel by this means.

Souls of other planetary systems have said they travel by thought. And, when they enter our dimension, by thought, they may manifest a spacecraft. They have very advanced technology like that we saw on the Star Trek episodes. They can travel by thought. They can indeed beam themselves to different locations. The technique uses *DNA and cell memory* and was compared to freeze drying food—the body cells are disassembled and then reassembled at the desired new location. Such advanced technology or information is only given to soul groups that are highly responsible, highly evolved, and highly developed spiritually. Souls of Earth are not that developed yet. *If all souls were highly evolved, a designated planet for learning emotions would not be necessary. If all souls were highly evolved spiritually, it would not be necessary for Earth to ever cleanse itself of contamination.*

Messengers also spoke of the electromagnetic field of the human body radiating out from the center or central core of the human body and a similar electromagnetic field has also been described for the axis of the

Earth. The messengers have stressed that, in order to channel, they must lower their energy vibration level to match ours. They also state that the human heart is the center for emotions. Their descriptions seem to align with the *Divine Matrix* descriptions of the energy field that surrounds the human heart. In that book, the image pictured on page fifty-one, figure two, was provided by the Institute of Heart Math. (Gregg Braden 2007)

Our Creator sent various souls to inform us that he keeps track of us through our DNA and cell memory that He/She placed in our soul cells. This is how He/She knows where we are, what we are thinking, and what we are experiencing at all times. This is how He/She knows our needs. He/She knows all there is to know about our souls, our thoughts, and our deeds of all the lives we have ever lived. This is repetitive by intention.

Also channeled repeatedly is how things work. The Creator is the purest energy and the highest of energy. *Whether that energy is behind a heart beating, or oxygen entering and exiting the lungs, or the energy connected to emotions and cells, or the ecosystems that support life on the Earth. The Creator's energy is the mix. This is an interactive system. We are like particles of the system. First came the planetary systems, then the* design of system occupants that could survive, reproduce and sustain themselves on what the environment provided. Once this was possible, then *Creator allowed souls with copies of His/Her own DNA and cell memory to enter the different forms they chose.* We do not see this because we are already part of the design. In essence, the Creator is the highest and purest of energy and we are all One because our souls contain His/Her DNA and cell memory.

These are the types of connections that Isaac Newton, Galileo, Edgar Cayce, Freud, Oshinbah, Celonious, Elijah and others are trying to have us understand. This is the energy field from which we were created and to which we return when we leave Earth. While working with channeled material, it has often been said to me: The hardest thing to learn is what you already know. I finally realized the speakers are referring to the fact a soul knows all of its history. When we need a bit of information stored there, the soul may provide that information to our present brain. Creator is the energy field of all that exists—all spaces seen and unseen and all that cannot be measured, weighed or placed on the slide of a microscope. Souls that channel who are closest to Creator say that they can't describe

Him/Her. Creator is perfect and only Creator is perfect. Also, most souls that channel have trouble describing what we would call a hierarchy of reporting or work task force. It is not all bliss and party time where they are. They work. They may make mistakes just as we do. They too are working back toward Creator.

Many of the famous people on Earth, such as Isaac Newton, Galileo, Freud and others, searched for answers as to how things work on Earth and in the universes. They were met with resistance or what was perceived as conflicts between science and religion. One conflict was when the soul enters the body. Some believe the body was created with a soul inside. Others believe that the body was created separately and the soul then enters. The latter is what was channeled. Also, other problems arose with the topics of religion and politics, and religion and education. Channeled material has often stated that Earth is the only planet with religion and time. Also, it is frequently channeled that Emperor Constantine had several books removed from the Bible and other things placed in the Bible that do not belong. At one time, people communicated directly with Creator and their needs were simply met through thought but the more humans evolved intellectually, the farther they grew away from direct communication with Creator and with God.

Indeed, there is an Energy Grid shaped very much like a spider web that covers and protects the Earth. Also, there are energy grids or pathways within us that connect us to the universal energy. In channeling, the Creator is described as the highest of pure energy—a vast energy bowl into which he continually creates and places universes, planetary systems, galaxies, planets and planet inhabitants. In channeling, messengers have described how we are connected by DNA and cell memory to the Creator.

In his book, *The Divine Matrix*, Gregg Braden explains that the book title refers to a form of "subtle energy" scientists had not known existed before. This energy does not work the way of a typical electrical field does. "Rather, it appears to be a tightly woven *web* and it makes up the fabric of creation" . . . one simple way to define the matrix is to "think of it three basic things: (1) a container for the universe to exist within; (2) the bridge between our inner and outer worlds; and (3) the mirror that reflects our everyday thoughts, feelings, emotions, and beliefs." He goes on to name the three attributes that set the energy of the matrix apart from other known energy are: "First it is everywhere, all the time . . . it already exists . . . Second, it appears that this field originated when creation . . . the beginning . . . The third characteristic, the one that makes it so meaningful to our lives, is that it appears to have "intelligence." In other words, the field *responds* to human emotion." Ibid.

In channeling, Edgar Cayce referred to an Energy Grid composed of love and white light that surrounds the earth. He noted that the grid serves the purpose of allowing Light Beamers of the galaxies to beam energy of love and White Light onto our planet. He indicated that the purpose for this is to protect us from dark energies, especially now, because the battle between good and evil is almost equal in strength. In addition, he and others have channeled that this is a special grid used only by those of Light. It enables those of other planetary systems that are assisting Earth to enter and leave.

Vehicles used by travelers from the far side of our galaxy touch the grid. The grid opens and, once the vehicle is through, the grid closes. It is like a net. Imagine a net or web that is ten feet wide and ten feet deep. A thirty-foot wide vehicle touches the web. The web expands to allow the vehicle to pass through. Then the web closes behind the vehicle. The web, vehicle and passengers remain invisible to the human. To remain invisible is an option. They may also appear as they truly are or as one of us. These beings are of White Light. Do not fear them.

Gregg Baden traces the history of the various theories behind the *Divine Matrix*. He wrote: The ancient collection of writings from India called the Vedas are among the world's oldest scriptures and are believed by some scholars to date as far back as 7,000 years." In one of the text, "the Rig Veda, there's a description of a force that underlies creation from which all things are formed—the force that was there before the beginning." This power, named Brahman, is identified as the "unborn . . . in whom all existing things abide." Further in the material it becomes clear that all things exist because "the One manifests as the many, the formless putting on forms." He goes on to say "in a different language, we could think of the Divine Matrix in precisely the same way—as the force before other forces. It's the container that holds the universe as well as the blueprint for everything that happens in the physical world . . . . This primal force of energy provides the essence of all that we experience and create. It holds answers to the questions about who we are. Ibid.

Braden wrote of two experiments involving DNA. The first experiment was by Vladimir Poponin a quantum scientist, and his colleagues, which included Peter Gariaev. They tested the "behavior of DNA on light particles (photons), the "stuff" of which our world is made. In short, the outcome of the experiment was these two statements: A type of energy exists that has previously gone unrecognized. And cells/DNA influence matter through this form of energy. Ibid.

In the 1990s, scientists working with the U.S. Army conducted tests to see the whether the power of our feelings, specifically DNA continues to have an effect when the cells are removed from the body. The condensed version of the test is that a swab tissue and DNA were collected from inside the mouth of a volunteer. The sample was isolated and taken to different area of the building. The donor remained several hundred feet away. While the donor was shown emotionally charged material of different types, the sample was measured electrically to see if it responded to the emotions of the person it came from. The results were yes. His cells and DNA showed powerful electrical responses at the same time that the donor was experiencing emotional stimulation by the images. The man who designed the experiment was Dr. Cleve Backster. "His pioneering work on the way that human intention affects plants had led to the military experiments." Ibid.

The military stopped their studies of the donor and his DNA. But the donor and his DNA remained in the same building as Dr. Backster. So, Dr. Backster and his team continued their studies. They separated the sample and donor by increasing distances and ran tests. The time between the donor's experience and the cell's response was measured by an atomic clock located in Colorado. "In each experiment the interval between the stimulus and response was zero—the effect was simultaneous. Ibid.

Braden in the summary of this experiment poses this question about organ transplants. If we can't separate people from the parts of their bodies, does this mean that when a living organ is successfully transplanted into another human being, the two individuals somehow remain connected to each other? Ibid.

The following excerpts are taken from the Gregg Braden website. Information printed on this site is from books by Gregg Braden. It is very much in line with what has been channeled by Naomi to me from various souls. For example, when this mission began, Jamiah and Elijah came and explained that Earth changes occur as ongoing cycles. Jamiah says woe unto those who do not heed the advice of the great I Am and follow the Golden Rule. Later, as we began to grasp their messages, we were told the cycles occur about every thirteen thousand years according to the Mayan Calendar, the equivalent of twenty-six thousand years of our calendar. The underlying cause of the changes is evil, dark energy. All souls contain the spark of the Creator. However, once created and approved to enter the Earth realm, some souls choose to go away from Creator. The farther away they stray, the darker they become. They are given numerous changes to return to Creator but most do not.

Chief White Feather and Jamiah once came and explained that some of the problems that have occurred in the state of New York and other areas are because of the original mistreatment of the American Indians. They specifically mentioned the word Manitoba. Jamiah said if the men who came to settle the area had used their knowledge to become friends instead of enemies, our country would be totally different today. Chief White Feather stated that, instead of becoming friends, one error begat another error and the spirit world knew this was an error. Since that time, to make amends, everyone has been allowed to enter our country.

More recent channeling states the Indian Nations have endured and tolerated much mistreatment. However, their leaders have the ability to see into the future and guide them. They know what is to come. They know that the Earth changes are imminent. They have no fear because they understand that life is a continuum and they will be rewarded and happy.

On his website: "As Gregg describes the Hopi diagram of life, there are two parallel paths. The upper path turns into a zigzag that ends nowhere. Those who choose this path are represented with their heads detached from and hovering above their bodies. They will experience the great shift as a time of confusion and chaos leading to destruction. The lower path continues as a level line, strong and even. Those choosing this path live to advanced ages and their crops grow strong and healthy. (http://www. mindbridge-loa.com/Bregg-Braden.html)

According to Gregg Braden, we are able to cross from one path to the other freely until the choice point two-thirds of the way along. There is, at that point, a vertical line connecting the two. From that point on a choice will have been made and there will not be another chance to change from one path to the other. Gregg quotes the prophecy, "If we hold fast to what the sacred was as he (the Creator) devised it for us, what we have gained, we will never lose." We only have to choose between the two ways . . . ."When earthquakes, floods, hailstorms, droughts, and famines will be the life of every day, the time will have then come for the return to the true path." Ibid.

Hopi elders believed that the severity of the cleansing is determined. The phenomenal events in the world around us test the belief systems of individuals and entire populations. The prophecy promises that the final three shakings will depend on "which path humans will walk: the greed, the comfort, and the profit, or the path of love, strength, and balance." Ibid.

"With the recent elections in the United States, it seems that Americans who choose balance are standing up to those who choose fear and self interests. This is a path that will help us to move off the path leading to destruction, to the path of abundance for all." Ibid.

Gregg Braden traveled the world gathering information for the *Divine Matrix.* He spent time in monasteries in China, Egypt, Bolivia, and Peru because they have kept in touch with the divine matrix. This was part of our culture also until it was edited out of our Biblical text in the fourth century. When Braden began studying the Dead Sea Scrolls, he found that we once had as part of our history the same teachings that he was only finding in these out-of-the-way places. Afterwards, their practices began to seem very strange to westerners. We called them primitive practices. Ibid.

Greg Braden says that is believed that the divine matrix was birthed simultaneously with the birth of our universe. When our universe had expanded to the size of a green pea, and was at about a billion, billion degrees, this divine matrix was carried with the expansion. Gregg says that the divine matrix is a bridge between our inner experiences, feeling, emotion and belief, and our outer worlds. Ibid.

The matrix carries everything from our healing, to the peace or violence in the world around us. It is also a mirror using the quantum essence of the stuff around us, of what we claim to be real. The divine matrix is literal. It will mirror back to us our beliefs and feelings about our relationships, checkbooks and our relation to our communities. The ancient texts encourage us to feel our feelings as if our prayers have already been answered. When we ask for healing of our loved ones we are acknowledging that an illness exists. Instead, the correct way to do this is to act as if the healing already occurred and rejoice, feel the gratitude. Ibid.

The Divine Matrix is the conduit that carries our conscious awareness out from our physical bodies. There is a quality of human emotion, a shift in perception that impacts the stuff in this divine matrix to conform to what we have in our hearts. It is not possible to exit from it. Every cell in our bodies is already submerged in this matrix. Gregg Braden explains that it would be impossible to hold our bodies together without it. If we are conscious, we are always interacting. We create through the power of human emotion. Ibid.

Our Bible has been revised many times and many sections have been removed completely. The "Bible says: Ask and she shall receive. Jesus actually said: Be surrounded or enveloped by your own desire so that your joy can be full . . . . Be this way, as if these things have already happened." . . ."The matrix is unbiased. It mirrors back to us what we create in our lives. Our thoughts imagine what we would like. Our hearts breathe life into this when powered by our feelings. The Nicean Council removed these sections from the Bible." Ibid.

Human feeling and human belief are the language of reality creation. As different as the various religious beliefs are today, if you trace them back to before there were religions, they were more similar in practices. Ibid.

The self-empowering books in the Bible were the ones taken out in the fourth century at the Nicean Council. The power of human emotions to rearrange the atoms and to interrupt the flow of time and space—this was in the descriptions of the books taken out of our traditions, although this was never taken out of other traditions, such as Native American and those living in Peru and in the Andes. The original Aramic was what told humans how to do these things. Ibid.

In our Book of Genesis, there is one line on the creation of the human being. In the original, there were many pages; our souls were created separate from our bodies. The original body could not contain the light and power of the soul and had to be redesigned. The original intent was to share the wisdom. Ibid.

The intent of the council was political. In the letters of some of the Bishops, they questioned this editing and deletion. Ibid.

Our science is showing that when we have strong feelings, not only are there changes inside our bodies, but also, there are changes outside of our bodies. The world around us is primarily electrical and magnetic. In our bodies, the largest generator of the electrical and magnetic divine matrix is the human heart. It has two times the power of the brain to create an electrical field and over one thousand times the power of the brain to create a magnetic field. Ibid.

The Language of the Heart is where the power is packed to change our future. Even though people are made aware of the truth the beliefs they have or the influences of the family and friends may impair their use of the matrix principles. Ibid.

Brandon Bays, author of The Journey, described her battle with self and a tumor. A most interesting encounter she had was at a seminar of Masters in the field of healing. She spoke with Deepak Chopra with whom she had a prior acquaintance. At the seminar Dr. Chopra spoke of a heart transplant patient who upon awakening from the surgery had the urge for

"Chicken Nuggets and fries even though she did not like them . . . Dr. Chopra explained that the "phantom memories" got passed on from one cell generation to the next. He went on to say that the various organs of the body regenerate at different speeds. The liver takes six weeks to regenerate, whereas the skin cells take only three to four weeks. A whole new stomach lining develops in only four days and all your eye cells replicate every two days. (Brandon Bays 2002)

Dr. Chopra asked, "If you get a whole new liver every six weeks, why is it that if you have liver cancer in January, it's still there in June . . . Your liver has regenerated itself several times by then. He went on to explain that stored inside our cells are old memories—he called them "phantom memories." These old patterns can eventually cause degenerative disease patterns within the cells. And before a diseased cell dies, it passes its memory onto the next cell being born. So the disease pattern continues. Ibid.

Dr. Chopra compared "the human body to a computer, saying it was possible to interrupt the programming, and that once the programming was interrupted, the possibility for healing existed. He intimated that in order to interrupt the programming, and uncover the cell memories and let them go, you would need to get in touch with the same part of you that had created the programming in the first place—the infinite intelligence, the body wisdom. And he suggested that those people who know how to get in touch with this body wisdom—to get the "Gap," the quantum soup, etc—these were the successful of survivors of disease.

He suggested that it was his observation that everyone got there in his or her own way. Some did it spontaneously and some by choice. He suggested it was part of the quantum mechanics of the way the body healed. Ibid.

After this information was given, Brandon Bays eventually designed methods of addressing her own problems and published her book in which she shares her experience of what worked and what did not.

Methods of clearing cell memory problems have been channeled. They are very simple. They require sincerity, commitment, and a desire to release the memory. Depending upon the depth of trauma felt and recorded, release of this memory may be a life changing experience. Clearing cell memory heals the wounded soul. As a result, the related physical condition usually heals. Edgar Cayce has repeatedly channeled that the soul must heal before the body heals.

Not all cell memories are negative. Our cells also record happiness, joy, love, habits, choices we have made etc. So, when we do exercise to clear negative cell memories, we also specify that we are keeping cell memories that are positive and helpful to us.

9

Cell Memory Clearing Procedure

Recently, Makala (who reports to Mother God and Creator) reminded me that when we are working with the cell memory clearing techniques such as dreams, meditation and hypnosis we are working with the soul. It is important to repeat this message: The soul *can override* the physical cell memories. The soul is still connected to Creator. Use your brain to tell your soul to override the traumatic cell memories. You must get to the part of you that created the problem and release the problem. The soul heals then the body heals.

In my own experience of working with cell memory, I experienced the worst low back pain of my life after a session in which Elijah spoke of the Civil War. He said the times in which we are currently living are comparable those of the Civil War. Jamiah later explained that my pain was cell memory, which was activated by the mention of the Civil War. Jamiah stated that I had been Captain Nathan Forbes. My horse was shot out from under me. I spent eighteen hours dying penned under the horse. I have heard the words Civil War many times. Why would this time have triggered the cell memories to manifest the onset of pain? Apparently, it was my age and the thoughts by Elijah comparing the present time we are living to conflicts of the Civil War era.

Elijah returned and specified steps to take to clear the cell memories permanently. (The incident and instructions for clearing the memory are recorded in my book *Heroes Without Halos* on pages 190-192). The more clearly you state the problem the faster the clearing. *This is not a game. Do not treat this as a game.*

Guidelines: Know, Understand and Accept These

These cell memories are memories recorded in your soul of real experiences that you have had.

The soul knows all of your thoughts, all your lives ever lived and every aspect of you.

You soul can override the physical body cell memories.

The Soul can override present life cell memory traumas and prior life cell memory traumas, which you do not recall.

Cell memory traumas of this life alone or combined with prior life stored memories may be wreaking havoc in your present life. These you are releasing.

You are retaining all cell memories that you have learned in the present life and all other lives that are of support and assistance to you.

Your brain is a computer gateway and coordinator between your soul and your emotions. How your react to the trauma and emotional upsets determines what gets stored as trauma.

Now, when you practice release of cell memory, you are telling your soul to release and clear the cell memory stored in the cells of your physical body. Read this carefully and understand clearly what I am writing.

What are you using? Your brain is your computer that is coordinating this activity. Your mind must *intend to release the problem.* You must understand that you physical body is a house or vehicle in which the soul resides.

The origin of this soul is from Creator and contains the same cell DNA and cell memory Creator originally placed there. Know that when you leave Earth—this same soul DNA will pull with it this same soul cell memory—from your physical body.

Also, know this: Your very essence is this same soul DNA and cell memory. When this soul gets to its destination after the physical dies, then this same soul DNA and cell memory are a record of the life you just lived. This is all that remains of the life just lived; and you will review it in the presence of the Creator's Energy, which is your origin. You will decide if you adhered to the contract that you—in the presence of the Council requested and got approved. If you arrive with cleared cell memories, your cleansing process is much faster than if you arrive with lots of "baggage."

Clearing Procedure

Select a quiet place to practice daily or a few times daily. You must be sincere and practice regularly. This may take several weeks to accomplish. Much depends on the degree of trauma, how long you have carried it and your willingness to let it go. Also, this exercise or meditation may be done anywhere, sitting in a chair, on the floor in the Lotus Position (with the feet and ankles crossed, and hands on the knees), in the shower or sitting in a warm bath.

If sitting in a chair is your choice, place both feet flat on the floor with hands relaxed on the lap. Look upward slightly and close your eyes. Relax your neck. Take slow deep breaths in and out through the nose. As you breathe slowly relax. Relax the face, the shoulders, the chest, hips, thighs, calves and feet. Let all tension release. *Remember that mind follows breath*. Relax. Breathe slow deep breaths.

In your mind, think of the purest blue water ever made by Creator or God or whatever name you call a higher power. (We are all One). Envision the water powering onto the top of your head and flowing completely down your back, legs, and feet. See the water flowing through your body and all the cells all the way through the tips of your toes.

In your mind say: I release to Creator or God this cell memory problem of my present life so that no harm is caused to myself or anyone else. *State the problem* (if known) as clearly as possible. For example, I release resentment. I release fear of horses and fear of abandonment. Also state: I *retain* all cell memories that are helpful and supportive of me in this present life.

If the *problem is not known*, then say: Even though I am not aware of prior life memories, I release all negative prior life cell memories that are harmful in my present life. I retain all prior life cell memories that are supportive and helpful to me in the present life. Thank you. Always give thanks to all who help you.

You may also practice this cell memory clearing in the shower or while sitting in a tub of water. In this case, visualize the water cleansing your cells as the shower pours pure clear water from the top of your head, through your cells and out through your feet. Or if you sit in a bathtub, just relax and focus on releasing.

I asked Elijah how do I know that I am free of a negative cell memory. He replied: It will not longer bother you. This proved to be true. Around August 2007 more negative cell memories emerged. (These were covered in *Awakening of the Soul*). These were of my late mother. I did not know that any existed but she knew that a tiny negative something remained. Repeatedly, it has been given that we must clear and forgiveness is often a big step in clearing. I used the technique above to clear this and other events also. This worked for me and it must be repeated several times to work. When you no longer think about it, you know it has worked.

Recently I heard a famous doctor on television state that a similar program is being taught to soldiers with amputated legs. They are taught techniques of meditation and visualization to relieve phantom limb pain.

10

Hypnosis

Hypnosis is a method recommended to clear traumatic memories. I highly recommend the book *Same Soul, Many Bodies* by Brian L Weiss, M.D. Dr. Weiss, a graduate of Columbia University and Yale Medical School, is Chairman Emeritus of Psychiatry at the Mount Sinai Medical Center in Miami. The book is full of information. In this book, Dr. Weiss expressed his belief that we are all immortal, meaning that our souls are immortal. The soul leaves the body and returns time after time. He stated that, "Dr. Sigmund Freud described the mind as functioning on different levels. Among them is what he called the unconscious mind, of which we are not aware, by definition, but which stores all our experience and directs us to act as we do, think as we do, respond as we, feel as we do. Only by accessing the unconscious, he saw, can we learn who we are and, with that knowledge, be able to heal. Some people have written that is what the soul is—Freud's unconscious." Dr. Weiss, through his own experience tends to agree. He stated that in his work of regressing souls to prior lives and more recently, progressing souls to future lives, he has helped people with problems heal. (Brian Weiss 2004)

Dr. Weiss explained the process of hypnosis and that the patient is always in control. The goal of hypnosis is to access the subconscious mind. The goal of meditation is the same. "The subconscious is not limited by our imposed boundaries of logic, space, and time." When you are hypnotized you are not asleep. Your mind is always aware of what you are experiencing while you are hypnotized. You can still talk, speak, comment, and criticize. Ibid.

In the hypnotized state the patient is regressed to different periods of time and he or she then reveals what he or she sees there. They describe what they see and what trauma occurred in that life. Once they see the events of their prior lives, they make the connection with the impact that life is having on the present live. After the sessions they often have a different outlook on their life and their problems. They eventually work through the problem and let it go. Ibid.

Some of the cases, under hypnosis, looked backward in time for hundreds of years and viewed the lives they lived. Some were ruthless and barbaric in one or more lives. In lives, that followed, *they realized they were working on issues they created by being heartless and barbaric. Some had committed rape and murder. Some had been forced to be caretakers. Some had been abusive spouses and of course some had been the recipients of spousal abuse.* Ibid.

Dr. Weiss stated: "When my patients remembered themselves in their other lives, the traumas that had brought them to me in the first place were eased and in some cases cured. That is one of the soul's primary purposes: to progress toward healing. Ibid.

Dr. Weiss goes on to point out that "Buddhists and Hindus have been accumulating past life cases for thousands of years. Reincarnation was written of in the New Testament until the time of Constantine, when the Romans censored it. Jesus himself may have believed in it, for he asked the Apostles if they recognized John the Baptist as Elijah returned; Elijah had lived nine hundred years before John. It is a fundamental tenet of Jewish mysticism; in some sects it was standard teaching until the early nineteenth century." . . . . Dr Weiss stated that he believes that "reincarnation is real . . . . That is our immortality." Ibid.

To assist your own healing Dr. Weiss gave directions on how to speak to yourself. To start, you must be deeply relaxed.

Pick only one mental or physical symptom that you want to understand. This issue could be a joint problem, a fear of falling, or obesity or anything you choose. The idea is to let your thoughts tell you what you think and feel about the issue. Be honest with yourself. "*Then switch places with the symptom.* You are the symptom, the symptom is you. This is so you can be most fully aware of the symptom. It knows where it is located and how it is affecting the mind and body. Next, have the you that is outside the symptom, ask the symptom a series of questions:

How have you affected my life?

What are you going to do with my body and mind now that you are in it?

How have you affected my relationships?

Do you help convey something that I cannot convey without you—a message or information?

Do you protect me from anyone or anything? Ibid.

During hypnosis, Dr. Weiss also progressed patients into the future following the present life. I personally found this fascinating.

One client he called Max found himself in a future life as a "teacher of many healers, a physician of the near future, surrounded by his students in a kind of celestial amphitheater."

He liked the work and he was teaching students "how consciousness separates from the body so we can understand the mechanisms of spiritual healing."

He said: "Consciousness is in stages. First it hovers over the physical body, reviewing its emotional life and preparing to go higher. Then it leaves the emotional body behind as well, all the while becoming lighter and lighter. In this state, I call it mental." Ibid.

Later he said: "When we understand how the four stages interact and affect each other, clues to psychological and bodily healing on the physical plane can be discovered, analyzed and applied." Ibid.

Dr. Weiss commented that what this client stated verified the vision of other clients so clearly that he recognized it . . . . Also, "what he saw tied to others' near death experiences, but he went further, to a place where he could talk about human consciousness and see it climbing toward the One." Ibid.

In this book, Dr. Weiss presents many cases of hypnotic regression and progression. In each one a related emotion or problem is named, defined and interpreted in easily understood terms. Compassion, empathy, endurance, tolerance, attitude and behavioral changes, are all prominent features. In addition, Dr. Weiss presents himself as a very understanding, spiritual person that shares his beliefs and knowledge.

Destiny of Souls by Dr. Michael Newton is another marvelous book. Dr. Newton holds a doctorate in Counseling Psychology and is a certified Master Hypnotherapist. He developed his own age regression techniques to take subjects under hypnosis beyond past life memories to more meaningful soul experiences between lives. He presented over sixty cases of hypnosis that he describes in detail. He presents various aspects of development of the souls and whether they are new beginning souls or souls that have reached advanced levels. During hypnosis, some beginner souls remember and provide information regarding their origin. The following few lines are quotes taken by Dr. Lipton from two beginner souls:

> "My soul was created out of great irregular cloudy mass. I was expelled as a tiny particle of energy from this intense, pulsating bluish, yellow and white light. The pulsations send out hailstorms of soul matter. Some fall back and are reabsorbed but I continued outward and was being carried along with others like me. The next thing I knew, I was in a bright enclosed area with very loving beings taking care of me. I remember being in a nursery of some sort where we were like unhatched eggs in a beehive. When I acquired more awareness I learned I was in the nursery world of Uras. I don't know how I got there. I was like an egg in embryonic fluid waiting to be fertilized and I sensed there were many other cells of young lights who were coming awake with me." More statements reveal that these souls received loving care from nursery mothers who opened their sacks and took care of them. (Michael Newton 2000)

Case 26 was of great fascination to me. This case has to do with the creating of new soul and the care they receive. Excerpts from Case 26, a woman named Seena. The woman was a specialist with children in the present world and in the spirit world. In the present world she works through hospice with severely ill children. In a past life, she was Polish but not Jewish and volunteered to enter a German internment camp in 1939. She did this to be near and help the Jewish children any way possible. She could have left the camp early on but later, it was impossible to leave. So she died in the camp. Ibid.

Under hypnosis, Dr. Newton asked Seena the most significant experience between her lives. She replied without hesitation.

"I go to the place of . . . hatching—where souls are hatched. I am an Incubator Mother, a kind of midwife. She confirmed that this was a type of soul nursery. "We help the new ones emerge. We facilitate early maturation . . . by being warm, gentle and caring. We welcome them. Ibid.

When asked, she described her surroundings in the nursery. She described that it's . . . gaslike . . . a honeycomb of cells with swirling currents of energy above. There is intense light.

. . . She confirmed that the structure is a honeycomb like structure but the nursery itself is "a vast emporium without seeming to be limited by outside dimensions. The new souls have their own incubator cells where they stay until their growth is sufficient to be moved away from the emporium." The Incubator Mother first sees the souls in the delivery suite. The suite is part of the nursery. "The newly arrived souls are conveyed as small masses of white energy encased in a gold sac. They move slowly in majestic, orchestrated line of progression toward the Incubator Mothers. Ibid.

Dr. Newton asked from where do they come. Seena replied: "At the end of the emporium under an archway the entire wall is filled with a molten mass of high-intensity energy and . . . vitality. It feels as if it's energized by an amazing love force rather than a discernible heat source. The mass pulsates and undulates in a beautiful flowing motion. Its color is like that on the inside of your eyelids if you were to look through closed eyes at the sun on a bright day." Ibid.

Seena describes the birth as "from the mass a swelling begins, never exactly from the same site twice. The swelling increases and pushed outward, becoming a formless bulge. The separation is a wondrous moment. A new soul is born. It's totally alive with an energy and distinctness of its own." Ibid.

Dr. Newton inquired as to what else Seena saw. She said that beyond the mass "she saw beatific glow of orange-yellow. There is a violet darkness beyond, but not cold darkness . . . it is eternity. Upon prompting, Seena said that she saw five other mothers there and she described that the responsibilities of the Incubator Mothers. "They hover around the hatchlings so we can . . . towel-dry them after opening their gold sacs. Their progression is slow because this allows us to embrace their tiny energy in a timeless, exquisite fashion . . . . The towel drying was clarified as a form of hugging. Ibid.

Seena described the appearance of the soul as white at first. Then upon a closer look, she noted the colors blue and violet glowing around them . . . an umbilical . . . the genesis cord of energy, which connects each one. She described the new souls as rather like a string of pearls on a silvery conveyer belt. Ibid.

Dr. Newton asked: "Does each new soul have an individual character at this point? Do you add or subtract from its given identity?" Ibid.

Seena answered, "No, this is in place upon arrival, although the new soul does not yet know who they are. We bring nurturing. We are announcing to the hatchling that it is time to begin . . . to awaken. We bring to the soul an awareness of its existence . . . ."The material continues on to reveal more details of the early soul. No two souls are alike and they do not begin incarnating for quite awhile. The soul is nurtured and thoroughly prepared before it is allowed to start incarnating. Seena also revealed that there are several places similar to Earth. Ibid.

I was attracted to Case 26 because it described the birth of a soul. I had never heard this before. It did remind me that Emma, my mother, once channeled how souls are regressed on the Other Side before they are born. She was temporarily assigned there. Naomi's mom works there also. She apparently chose this as an assignment.

I thoroughly enjoyed reading the numerous cases Dr. Michael Newton presented in this book. I still have a few more to read.

Conclusion

In channeling, I was repeatedly told that *Beyond Cell Memory* is the last of three books that I contracted to write. I agreed to write these books before I came to Earth. In dreams, they have been shown to me in the Hall of Records. The overall purpose in writing the books was to assist people during Earth changes and after Earth changes. People will lose family members, homes and cherished belongings. Some people will have serious injuries and traumas. The primary purposes behind these channeled books are: to help people understand what happened—many will not understand and children will not remember; to help people understand their true origin and how to use the soul to heal cell memories; and to relay messages about emergency supplies and locating safe areas.

For many years, we have repeatedly heard that the earth was changing. Also, we have heard that the Earth would end on a certain day. I have not been told that. Perhaps the Earth will be retired to restore itself, as was Mars.

I have been told that the Earth is cleansing itself of contamination and of evil or dark souls. Thereafter, "Earth will have a newness." Only Creator, the highest and purest of all that exists, knows when events will occur. The one thing declared for certain in the books is that, life on Earth is like a three act play. Act I seems to have begun around World War I. Over the years that followed, we prospered and grew. We kept Creator and God in our midst—in our governments, on our money, in our schools, and in our homes. We had United States.

In more recent years, things began to change. Earth became more and more contaminated, and people became more filled with greed and driven by the acquisition of things and money. These were our big errors. Meanwhile, technology enabled the world to exchange information in seconds. Morals were replaced with greed when such things as giant company executives raped the investors. Many companies and world leaders lost credibility. Trust was lost. Still, few leaders are trusted now.

To make matters worse, terrorists, using our own airplanes filled with innocent passengers, killed around three thousand people on 9/11/2001. The channeled book *Heroes Without Halos* followed. It spoke of how things work on the Other Side, how the people crossed over, and gave special messages to the families of victims. More victims continue to die from this massacre because of the toxins inhaled and released into the air. Hundreds of people are still suffering and gradually dying from conditions caused from this event. Hundreds of others are monitored for evidence of disease by regular testing. This heinous act opened the door for Earth cleansing. *This door will not be closed.*

The second book *Awakening of the Soul* is filled with more detailed material of how things really work, what disasters are to come, and what measures to take. Our world is often looked upon as a play and each person or group has a role to play. Most recently, it was stated in channeling that the death of Bin Laden was the close of Act II. *So, we are well into Act III, the final act. It is in preparation for the end of this act that Beyond Cell Memory is written.*

As stated in the beginning, by those sent by Creator to speak through Naomi, Creator sent them to tell us the truth of our origin. He, in simple words, had Jamiah and others state that he created each soul from one of his own cells. Each soul has the DNA and cell memory of the Creator—an exact copy. He also explained how our physical bodies were created and how and when our souls enter the bodies. We were told that no two souls are alike.

Celonious was sent to explain to us: how our charts are created and approved on the Other Side; how we recognize what our soul needs to learn in order to grow; and how we choose to experience specific things in order to learn these needed lessons.

We were repeatedly told that opportunities to grow are placed in our paths. We have the opportunity to choose to like all people regardless of race, creed, color, sexual preference or national origin. We must not judge others because we each have experienced being all different nationalities, religions, statuses, and different planetary systems. We must not cause harm to the soul of another or force our beliefs onto anyone. We are all leaning at our own pace.

Also, be clear on this point. We have been taught wrong on many things. We are expected to be patient, tolerant and endure. However, we are not expected to tolerate emotional or physical abuse, neither or we to give it.

We have been informed that the homosexual person is simply balancing the masculinity and the femininity of the soul. We all must be balanced to return to Creator. Also, having someone homosexual for a neighbor or in your family is an opportunity to get to know and care for another soul. In another life, you may have been prejudice and now is your opportunity to overcome that. In another life, you may have been homosexual.

We were also informed that abortion is acceptable under some conditions. Abortion is especially approved in situations where the mother is not ready or the baby is not ready. We are not to judge this mother and she is not to suffer guilt.

Suicide is not an approved way to exit and is dealt with sternly. However, the situation of the soul is understood. The soul receives help and eventually, must still complete the contract it was supposed to have completed. It was stated that when someone commits suicide, he or she knows immediately that the act of suicide was a mistake.

We have covered organ transplants, a subject I knew nothing about when I started this project. I now feel fairly well informed. We have been told that it is possible to decrease organ rejection by preparing the recipient's mind to accept the organ, and to understand cell memory clearing. Understanding reincarnation or believing in reincarnation assists the recipient to accept the organ.

In Part III, you find dreams and how to encourage dreaming. Also, you have information and procedures to clear traumatic cell memories. There is no one method to cure all problems. *Meditation and cell memory clearing may become successful in relief of phantom limb pain suffered by amputees.* Acceptance and practice of cell memory clearing are keys to success. Hypnosis may be the best solution for the most difficult cases, such as people have lived a lifetime of abuse and extreme traumas. Whatever the issue, clearing the cell memory while you are on this side is strongly advised because it is much easier and much quicker to accomplish.

Clearly, our Earth is rapidly moving toward cataclysmic events, as I write. The Mississippi River is presently flooding and will continue over the next few days. Several southern states have been declared disaster areas since record-breaking tornadoes recently destroyed property and killed around 350 people. Many are still missing.

What we are observing and experiencing is like a preview of what is to come. Learn to breathe slowly and calm the mind. This helps in times of stress. Also, how you go through trauma determines whether it ends up being a cell memory that requires release later. This book is to help you clear cell memories of emotional traumas. Many traumatic events will occur as we go through the upheavals of Earth changes.

Creator sent Makala to give this closing information. Your current top leader will remain through the Earth changes and help lead people of the world after the changes. He charted and volunteered to this. His preparation as a child and as an adult prepared him for this role. Some people do not perceive him favorably. Some may try to remove him from office. This will not occur. The cataclysmic event will occur first. He and his family are of the White Light and among the very highest spiritually.

A certain percentage of those humans were scheduled to stay here and be a part of the new Earth after the Earth changes. But allowing fear and dark energy to take over and control removes them from Earth. So, they will be departing. In other words, what you are being given is this: Those who were appointed to stay or chose to stay on, when they submit to fear, and submit to dark energy, then their charts are changed and they will be removed and gone from Earth.

You must have in those left on Earth those who had faith in and knew what was happening and stuck with it, because they will be the survivors, the ones that construct or reconstruct. You will be led by the mightiest of the Rainbow Children that Creator had. I say had because they are now here on Earth. They are now many of the grandchildren that belong to those of you on Earth. Different little people that appear to be too aggressive or too knowledgeable are also those who will be leading. Little people will be those who are leading.

That is difficult for some adults to understand because they don't feel these children—and they will be children in size—have the ability to lead or should be recognized as leaders. But, I am coming to you today because Creator wants you to know that they are highly capable of leading. They have been patient and dilly-dallying around with human things waiting for this event. They may walk up to you or other survivors and say: The thing to do in this case. Listen to them they know. If they say to you there is food over here and a place to dwell, and your mind is saying no, go with them anyway. They have intuitive abilities that are beyond any on Earth at this time. They have used it somewhat since they came but it will be opened after the Earth changes occur.

This is important for you to know. Otherwise, there will be rejection of these souls unless this is given. Somehow this message must given to the people. Share this with others if you wish. Creator would like others to know.

Makala: The transition will be easy. It will be disturbing, a sort of trauma with the waters emptying. But after that and everything clearing, it is not describable. There will be total peace and nothing but love. The energy being positive all the time allows you to step forward and carry through and survive with ease. You do not have any complications. If you say: I have need of food, food will arrive; or I have need of water, water will arrive.

Do not question this because it will appear. Understand that energy it is there now on Earth for this to happen, but it is overridden by the negative. The negative energy will be gone. There will be direct communication with Creator and angels and all of us on this side. Now, we will not come down delivering food, it will not be as that. What you need will arrive.

Now, many of you have stored and prepared and that is wise but many are not prepared. Some think they are prepared and are not. Sickness and illness will not exist. Should one have temporary periods of not feeling well, you have energy workers that can come and transmit immediately their healing energy into you. It is a paradise to look forward to. It is a unique opportunity to experience, as no other has been. So, do not dread it. Do not fear it. The word fear has disqualified many souls from staying here. Creator disqualifies those souls. Even though you wrote in your chart that your were going to do this, Creator seeing dark energy within a soul, will remove the soul from Earth so that it may go through the purifying process and they will not be returned to Earth. They had their opportunity to stay strong. They chose not to, or perhaps they were overwhelmed. That is not a judgment call.

I feel, as I am delivering these messages, a strength that I have never had. It is overwhelming to feel the energy and know that I am feeling what will be after the changes. This is a very grand opportunity for me to give this information. Be sure to give this as information delivered by Makala from Creator. Thank you for this opportunity to give information. End

I hope you find this book helpful in the present and in the future that we face. Thank you for the opportunity to share what I have learned.

Grace J. Scott

Reference List

Part I. Origin, Purpose and Use of DNA and Cell memory

1. Jamiah: Creator—DNA and Cell Memory

Scott, Grace J. (2009). *Awakening of the Soul.* 648-651.

5. Edgar Cayce: Creator is Energy; DNA of Soul is Energy

Edgar Cayce: "Twentieth Century Psychic–Medical. Clairvoyant. Who Was Edgar Cayce?" (http://www.edgarcayce.org/are/edgarcayce.aspx). Accessed 6/1/2011.

Part II. DNA and Cell Memory Connections

2. Sir Isaac Newton: Cell Memory/Universe Connections

Isaac Newton Institute for Mathematical Sciences. "Isaac Newton's Life." (http://www.newton.cam.ac.uk/newtlife.html). Special thanks to the Microsoft Corporation for their contribution to our site. The information for the article came from *Microsoft Encarta.* Accessed 11/15/2006.

3. Galileo: Cell Memory, Math, Astronomy and Soul

Nova: "Galileo's Battle for the Heavens—His Place in Science." PBS. (http://www.pbs.org/wgbh/nova/galileo/science.html) "His Place in Science" by Dava Sobel. "His Telescope (and Sir Isaac's)" by Peter Tyson. Accessed 11/16/2006.

4. Dr. Freud: Introduction to Dream Work and Cell Memory
Freud, Sigmund. (http://www.nndb.com/people/736/000029649/)

7. Dr. Carl Jung: Homosexuality

Jung, Carl. "Personality Theories." By Dr. C. George Boeree. 1997, 2006. (http://webspace.ship.edu/cgboer/jung.html)

12. Transplants

Kline, Mitchell. Staff Writer. (2006). "A mother's gift Her 'babies' died; their organs let 9 live." *The Tennessean*. Volume 102. No 197. Sunday, July 16, sec. 1; A 8-9.

Pearsall, Paul, Ph.D. (1998). *The Heart's Code*. New York: Broadway Books. 88-91.

Pearsall, Paul, PhD., Gary E. Schwartz, PhD, Linda Russek, PhD. (2005). "*Organ Transplants and Cellular Memories*." Extracted from Nexus Magazine, Volume 12. Number 3. April-May. Accessed 3/1/2010. http://paulpearsall.com/info/press/3.html.

Silverstein, Amy. (2007). "*Trial by Transplant*." U. S. News and World Report. October 22. 46-50. Excerpt from: Amy Silverstein. *Sick Girl*. Grover Press.

Takeuchi, Leslie A. B. A., PTA., "Cellular Memory in Organ Transplants." San Francisco Medical Society. http://www.sfms.org. Accessed 2/28/2010.

(Takeuchi, a physical therapy assistant, is a graduate student in Holistic Health at John F. Kennedy University in Orinda, California. An article about Julie Motz's energy healing work appeared in the June/July issue of San Francisco Medicine in 2000. Her book, *Hand of Life*, was published by Bantam Books in 1998). Accessed 2/28/2010.

Part III. Use of DNA and Cell Memory

6. Organ Transplants: Issues and Concerns

Frist, William H., M.D. (1989). *Transplant*. New York: Ballantine Books.

8. Connecting the Dots

Braden, Gregg. (2007). *The Divine Matrix*. California: Hay House, Inc. 37-58.

Braden, Gregg. (2009). *Fractal Time*. California: Hay House.

Bays, Brandon. (2002). *The Journey*. New York: Simon & Schuster. 41-53.

Browne, Sylvia. Written with Lindsay Harrison. (2002). *Dreams*. New York: Dutton. 6-77.

Browne, Sylvia. (2000). *Soul's Perfection*. Carlsbad, California: Hay House.

Chopra, Deepak, M.D. (2000). *How to Know God*. New York: Harmony Books.

Chopra, Deepak, M.D. (2006). *Life After Death*. New York: Harmony Books. 222-224.

Degenhardt, Scott. (2005). *Surviving Death*. Tennessee: Scott Degenhardt.

Hicks, Esther and Jerry. (2006). *The Law of Attraction*.

Lumpkin, Joseph B. *The Gnostic Gospels of Philip, Mary Magdalene and Thomas*. Alabama: Fifth Estate.

Walsch, Neale Donald. (1999). *Friendship with God*. New York: Berkley Publishing Co.

Zukav, Gary. (1989). *The Seat of the Soul*. New York. Simon & Schuster.

Zukav, Gary. (2000). *Soul Stories*. New York: Simon & Schuster.

9. Cell Memory Clearing: Guidelines and Procedure

Cayce, Edgar. Edited and Arranged by Jeffrey Furst. (1972). *Edgar Cayce's Story of Attitudes and Emotions*. New York: Berkley Publishing Group.

Scott, Grace. J. (2009). *Awakening of the Soul*. New York: iUniverse. 1-13.

Scott, Grace J. (2008). *Heroes Without Halos*. iUniverse. New York. 190-193.

10. Hypnosis

Newton, Michael, Ph.D. (2000). *Destiny of Souls*. Minnesota: Llewellyn. 125-133.

Weiss, Brian, M.D. (2004). *Same Soul, Different Bodies*. New York: Free Press. 7-25, 47-48, 69-70.